D.L. BAILEY

DECENCY

AND

DECEPTION

Encouragement for a Struggling Nation

 FriesenPress

Suite 300 - 990 Fort St
Victoria, BC, V8V 3K2
Canada

www.friesenpress.com

ISBN
978-1-03-911806-5 (Hardcover)
978-1-03-911805-8 (Paperback)
978-1-03-911807-2 (eBook)

1. POLITICAL SCIENCE, POLITICAL PROCESS, ELECTIONS

Distributed to the trade by The Ingram Book Company

Contents

To God Almighty, and my Lord and Saviour Jesus Christ.

To my wonderful wife Elyse, and my two sons, Tsion, and Canaan, who inspired me to write my thoughts. Thank you!

To my closest and dearest friends, Paul and Cathy, Lance and Tracy

To my incredible parents Ron and Sarah. Christian, Husband and Father!!!

Introduction

I have had a passion for politics for many years. Following both Canadian and American political figures and having developed a great appreciation for those men and women who put themselves in position to make a difference in their community. I have worked on Canadian Federal and Provincial elections, spanning over 16 years. I have enjoyed the excitement of being part of a team working towards bettering our community. Working on campaigns brings you closer to the issues facing people in your community. Knocking on doors and sharing heartfelt moments with them creates an awareness of what policies are working and which ones are allowing some to be left behind. I have had the great fortune of working on many Leadership teams, with those men and women hoping to lead the Party to a brighter future. And the true honour of being elected to four terms as President of the Electoral District Association in my district. All those countless hours of talking to people about their concerns, and about their needs has been a great education for me. Watching how true leadership is done and what it looks like to put community first, has allowed me great insight into what we need as a game plan to successfully build the future. Passionate about politics in both Canada and the United States, I have watched closely what transpires when Republicans are in the White House and when Democrats are in the White House. Over the course of the last thirty-five years, I have witnessed a pattern of behaviours that I felt, needed to be addressed.

Understanding that we do not have to see eye to eye on all, or any policy, or figure's historical thumbprint, but need to showcase respect for each other. We must work to find common ground or find where we adamantly are not going to gain anything by further discussions. To only hear one side of an argument, or to surround ourselves with those people that tell us what we wish to hear, we sell ourselves short. The art of debate has become lost in today's world, and the ability to discuss subjects that maybe risqué, has literally filled our conscience with fear. This will lead to never resolving issues, or becoming informed on subjects we know little about, from people who have lived through historical events.

Changing our history and our failures of the past will only doom us to relive them. We must be bold, be courageous, but respectful always of others. This book is designed to outline and point out where I feel the largest failures have happened, where the people who had the opportunity to stand tall but left us wanting. Pointing out a difference in characteristics of people from the Left mostly that I feel acted to a lesser standard than I hold those on the Right to. This book is a formulation of my opinion of happenings, and events that has shaped my political view. It is meant to enlighten those of like mind and intrigue those of the Left that disagree with my opinion. I understand that the pressures of holding high office positions within Governing of countries is difficult on people. Therefore, this book is meant to highlight those people who acted poorly, or showcase how we have strayed from the values, and practices that have built North America so strong.

I hope to take you on a journey through events and happenings that shaped the period from 2016 to 2021. I hope to showcase where America has gone off the path that they had originally designed for their people. Perhaps offering a small insight into how voters can demand representation from their elected members that reflect accountability. Some aspects of today's political makeup I do not agree with, and some policies I do not think are strong. I mainly focus on the people involved in today's politics and discuss how they have performed in their roles.

I do reference remarks made by other people towards some of the figures I mention in this book. I do so to strengthen the point I am making about them performing in the role they have been given by the people. I neither agree or disagree with the remarks by others only highlight that my opinions are based on happenings and past experiences.

This book is designed to ask the questions of the reader, are we misinformed, are we being led astray, and are we able to get back to a time we have clearly left behind? You the reader can form your own opinion, you will quite definitely agree or disagree with my view, and hopefully be entertained in doing so.

Chapter One
The Clinton Run

Nearing the end of Barack Obama's second term as President of the United States, who would have guessed that Donald J. Trump would be his successor? From the wide selection of candidates vying for the Republican candidacy, Trump was not the favourite among political pundits, but he would eventually win the nod, and start his journey to the Oval Office. The Democrat opponent for the 2016 election is none other than Hillary Clinton, former first lady, former Secretary of State, and senator from New York. The hatred between Trump and Clinton seems to be only politically not overtly personal, but the disdain Trump showcases for her actions is palpable and is not at all hidden or cloaked. Hillary's run for President is not a smooth transition from her duties in Obama's administration to her campaigning across the nation. Before the end of her time as Secretary of State, Hillary would see accusations about her emails sent over nonsecure personal accounts, and her role in the deaths of four Americans in Benghazi. Her role in informing Americans that the deaths were over a movie and not a terrorist attack then answering, "what difference does it make?", would be front and centre for Donald Trump's team. Trump would coin the phrase crooked Hillary and try to showcase to America that Hillary was untrustworthy and that she had been part of the problem for so many years. How true was that depiction, is becoming more evident daily and now years later has become something we are still witnessing?

Let us break down some of those scandals and address them.

Email scandal where Hillary was caught using her personal devices to send information across non secure lines that contained sensitive information. It was concluded that, there was significant evidence that showcased that they were extremely careless in their handling of sensitive, highly classified information FBI Director Comey would state. There were over 110 emails containing classified information sent over non secure lines. Between what was turned over by the Clinton team and keeping in mind devices were literally smashed with a hammer or wiped clean, it lends to the conspiracy theories that Clinton is hiding the truth. A very frightening fact is how Hillary uses humor as an attempt to avoid answering questions about her emails. When asked by a Reporter in August of 2015 if she wiped her computer Hillary responded with a joke about using a cloth to clean it. And once on The Tonight Show she laughed off the question stating she is offended that her emails are boring. These actions of destroying devices, wiping devices, and not turning over all emails requested, did little to bolster her image leading up to the election in 2016. The fact that FBI director Comey did little after admitting that there was evidence of inappropriate handling of classified information, also a contributor to further tarnish Clinton's image.

Bernie Sanders was in the driver seat for a large portion of the Democrat nomination race. His team and message were resounding well with an ever-growing number of American, youth that were disenfranchised with the old system in Washington. Looking like Bernie could not be stopped the Clinton team started to become the favourite of the Democrat national committee members, and worked against Bernie, and those emails were released showcasing the prejudice in Clinton's favor. Bernie Sanders stated many times that he thought the DNC chair Debbie Washerman Schultz was working against him from the start. Now it is important to note those emails only came out through WikiLeaks and the DNC claimed that Russian hackers were the source. This would set the stage for Russian interference for the next few years ahead. Bernie would eventually step aside, and Hillary Clinton would be named the Democrat presidential candidate for the 2016 election.

Michael D. Shear and Matthew Rosenberg, (July 22, 2016). Released Emails Suggest the D.N.C. Derided the Sanders Campaign. https://www.nytimes.com/2016/07/23/us/politics/dnc-emails-sanders-clinton.html

Benghazi where four Americans died on the anniversary of September 11/01. On September 11, 2012, four Americans came under attack and died in Benghazi Libya at the US consulate. Ambassador Chris Stevens, information officer Sean Smith, and CIA operatives Glenn Doherty, and Tyrone Woods were killed in two attacks one at the consulate and the other at the safe house. The following investigation and answering before the 2013 Senate Foreign Relations Committee, Hillary Clinton would capture headlines for months. Clinton would be central to those questions and feeling the pressure of the situation did not answer those questions well. The now famous, "what difference does it make?", answer given by Clinton showcased her frustrations and was immediately perceived to be in poor, taste. When Senator Ron Johnson(R-WI), asked Hillary Clinton about the cause of the attack. The truth of the matter was not what caused the attack, but could it have been prevented, and whether it was a movie or a terrorist attack, four men were dead. There has been lots written about the Benghazi attack and if more could have been done to safeguard those American's, but the damage was done to Hillary Clinton's image already. It is not my intentions in this book to use these brave men and the loss of their lives, and the pain that their family must still feel to form opinions of Hillary Clinton or Barack Obama. I only wanted to showcase that some Americans held it against her, and that it hurt her chances of holding the highest office in the country.

With so many scandals already surfacing around Hillary Clinton you would think that playing by the rules very closely would be in her best interest. Going into the first debate between Donald

Trump and herself unbeknownst to the voting masses or to Trump, Hillary had been given the debate questions. Donna Brazil shared the questions and their subject matter with the Clinton campaign. Brazil would go on to say she regretted the action, and that it was just what the Russian hackers wanted to do, cause divide among the Democrat party. Again, this showcases a deflection of blame away from herself and onto the Russians just like Clinton did over the email scandal. Also, worth noting here is that there is a heavy Russian fear mongering being put forward by the Democrat party members, and that seems to be the birthplace of the Trump Russian collusion we would see for the next few years.

Donna Brazile, (March 17, 2017). Donna Brazile: Russian DNC Narrative Played Out Exactly As They Hoped. (http://time. com/4705515/donna-brazile-russia-emails-clinton)

Considering all these scandals, and the lack of judgment situations the damage that was done to Hillary Clinton's image was far worse than what her and her campaign team knew about. The lead up to election night was of course not without some moments of bolstering for the Clinton team. Trump was heavily attacked and mocked by mainstream media, and by Hollywood celebrities alike. Late Show hosts like John Oliver openly called on Trump too "do it". Mocking Trump as if he had zero chances and were salivating at the chance of using material in their shows. George Clooney answered questions from reporters was asked about Donald Trump winning the Presidency, stated there is not going to be a President Trump. Obama himself read mean tweets from Trump on Jimmy Kimmel and stated, "at least I will go down as a President". Heavy influence from a variety of sources designed to sway Americans in their perception of Trump and deflect away from some heavy damage to Clinton's image. Perhaps the most damning to Clinton's image was her refusing to say Donald Trump won the 2016 election and her call for uncivil behavior until the White House was one back. Hillary has stated she beat Trump already once, she could do it again in the lead up to the 2020 election. These instances both coming after the 2016 election loss were just an extension up Hillary's refusing to admit defeat. There is a very laughable undertone to Clinton refusing to admit that Donald Trump won, she previously asked Trump if he would concede once she had won and is now to this day still not doing what she has asked Trump. I think it is incredibly important to note that perception of a person is important, and that the image American voters form in their own minds is the most difficult task to predict during an election. Hillary Clinton lost credibility by involving herself in numerous scandals, and for some personal choices of saying whatever would win over the crowd she was addressing. Case in point, she was being interviewed on The Breakfast Club by two African American hosts, and when asked what is one, thing she keeps in her purse she responded with, hot sauce. They shared a laugh but when she was asked if she was pandering for black votes she asked, "is it working"? These situations led to Clinton being asked by Anderson Cooper if she is willing to say anything to get votes. The difference in leadership styles between Trump's very direct approach and Hillary's seeming to change her stance on the fly is very evident. Hillary would change her stance on policies she had endorsed before, find an accent when campaigning in the southern states, tarnished her believability with voters. It was beginning to look more like people were voting against Hillary more than they were voting for Donald Trump.

Chapter Two
Election Night

By the time, the day of election 2016 started the mainstream media and Hollywood celebrities alike had been in overdrive in support of the Clinton team. Many daytime talk shows were about the election and the possibility of Trump winning. No one had Trump coming out on top and most of the coverage was squarely on Clinton's historic vote as the first woman President. The day would not belong to Hillary Clinton. The more typical States going to Clinton, it was the blue wall States that Clinton would not spend time in during the campaign, that Trump went to, and eventually won that did Hillary in. One thing worth noting is how angry some mainstream media anchors became as Donald Trump numbers started to roll in. I feel it also worth noting that journalism has given way to a more lobbyist style coverage where news outlets are extremely partisan. Once the news was reported but now it seems that information is given in a way to form our opinions for us. I feel that the announcement of Donald Trump as the 45th President of the United States of America was the moment The Democrat party needed to finally end its Clinton ties and to finally close the book on Hillary's time in active politics. The party needed to heal some wounds caused by scandals, health questions, and trustworthy issues.

During the collection of exit poll numbers, it was starting to look like Hillary was about to have a landslide win. Some early numbers were showcasing a 92% to 8% lead for Hillary Clinton. Those exit poll numbers would be the talk of many mainstream media stories and talk shows alike and how could the numbers be so wrong or so far off. The main reason for the numbers being so far off is a new cultural behavior taking place across America. Tolerance is at an all time low, and Conservatives feel under attack often. Cancel culture is taking a firm grip on society. Standing outside of the polling stations were a few groups, one such group would be Black Lives Matter. BLM were more firmly behind the Clinton led Democrats and I think added to the wrong information being collected, and not being reliable or accurate. Confrontations before the election between Black Lives Matter, and Republicans wearing MAGA hats were all over YouTube. These confrontations would lead to people giving false statements exiting the voting polls in fear of such confrontations happening to them. More should be done to ensure voters feel safe at polling stations and only those people working during the election should be allowed where voters are. No groups should be allowed to confront or be present, to ensure everyone gets to vote safely.

The newest election tool utilized by both parties is the widespread reachability of social media. The problem with social media is there tends to be less accountability and facts are often inaccurate at best. This form of attacking your opponent is effective in a day and age where people are all too happy to have someone else tell them the quick version without fact checking. I also feel that the two sides are very much different in their approach to politics in the fact that the Right or Republicans tend to be very fact based where the Left or the Democrats tend to use feelings more so than facts. This is maybe what led Joe Biden to say, "we don't care about facts", once while giving a speech. Social media posts reflect this trend as well, we see where Republican memes tend to be rooted in actual happenings where Democrat memes are created to arouse an emotion. It was this emotional Democrat supporter base that had such a difficult time on election night and Hollywood celebrities were among this group. The panel on CNN and MSNBC were in shock, Van Jones called it a "white lashing", putting a negative spin on what America had ultimately decided they wanted as President.

Van Jones on a Trump win: This was a white lash. (Nov 9, 2016), Site name. (https://www.youtube.com/watch?V=MA9aSvHzEIU),

The next four years it seemed that no attack on Trump's character would be considered too far, or against his children, and wife. With perhaps the most beautiful and elegant first lady to ever live in the White House, Melania Trump was not given magazine covers, glowing stories, or invites to shows like The View, or many of the other things Michelle Obama was given. Joy Behar, Kathy Griffin, Robert DeNiro, Cher, and many other celebrities showcased hatred towards Donald Trump in various ways from posing with Trump's bloody severed head, to saying, "I would punch him in the face". The position Hollywood would take during Trump's four years would distance the American people even further from the elite of movieland, showcased by a lower viewership turning out for Oscar night and other award shows. The use of these award shows as a platform to promote The Democrat party is tainting the image of Hollywood even more in the mind of everyday America. Mark Wahlberg once said, Hollywood is out of touch with everyday America. More of Hollywood should come to this same conclusion.

The Electoral College is under attack from the Left, and they want to see it removed from use. This would be disastrous, as campaigning would focus on only a handful of States and the voice of so many Americans would go silent in its aftermath. Voters rights were something that not everyone enjoyed from the beginning, African Americans had to fight for those rights, women had to fight for those rights, so any kind of motion or proposal to go back to silencing votes is political control. The use of the Electoral College is why Hillary Clinton refuses to say she lost the election in 2016 to Donald Trump. The use of the Electoral College has been around since the 1800s so for Democrat governors to be pushing for the abolishment of the Electoral College hopefully will be to no avail. In 2016 The

American people would have their say they would officially close the door on Hillary Clinton being in the White House and America's first female President. They would put their faith in Donald J Trump to lead them back from Obama's policies on health care, homeland security, job creation, border security, and defending cheaper health-care. The wall on the southern border was very much being built, jobs came back to historically low unemployment, and insulin for diabetics came down in cost by hundreds of dollars which helped coin the phrase, "promise made promise kept".

Chapter Three
The Trip Up

Focusing on the transition now of the Obama White House to the Trump White House, that transition was not smooth. Trump becoming the President of the United States started on some heavy accusations from the Democrats and the mainstream media was there to promote those accusations. The media and most of the Left leaning daytime shows were in love with lawyer Michael Avenatti, who was representing adult actress Stormy Daniels, and her claim Trump paid her hush money. This love affair with Avenatti would lead to some Democrat supporters and media people hinting about Avenatti himself running for President against Donald Trump in 2020. Avenatti would have some very heated battles with Republicans and Donald Trump, himself claiming he would beat Trump and go on to win the White House. This played out long enough for Donald Trump's name to get used plenty of times in a negative light on every major media outlet. Avenatti was loving every minute of it, unfortunately for both Daniels and Avenatti the accusations were unfounded, and Daniels would be ordered to pay $300,000 in legal fees to Donald Trump. Michael Avenatti would end up being found guilty of extortion, domestic abuse, and other charges, and could face up to 40 years in jail. The stage would be set for the next four years, and it would get busy on the allegation front.

Trump would be attacked by MSNBC host Rachel Maddow and accused of not paying enough taxes. She would over the period of weeks do her show addressing the Trump tax returns trying to uncover a tax evasion of some sort. As the tax return would be shared on her show, which Trump's team stated was illegal, proving that Trump did in fact pay $38 million on an income of $150 million, much higher percentage rate than he needed to pay. The thing that is remarkable to me, Rachel Maddow did not open this return before going on air and spend any time or effort to ensure proof before trying to convince America there was a smoking gun within its envelope, only to be made to look petty and foolish live on air. She would end the reveal with a "mazel tov", to Trump for making $150M. The real problem is not what was inside that envelope potentially, it was that the mainstream media used yet another situation, real or fake, to further erode the image of Donald Trump. Revealing to most on the Right what the real game plan is of the Left. Trump would again be asked to reveal his taxes before the 2020 election to a lesser degree.

Exclusive Look At President Trump's 2005 Tax Return | Rachel Maddow | MSNBC. (Mar 14, 2017), Site name. https://www.youtube.com/watch?v=0eB-xjDMGdQ

Leading up to the 2016 election the Democrats would have to admit that Russian hackers did breach the server of the Democrat National Committee. Wikileaks would release information that the Democrats were working against Bernie Sanders, and that Hillary Clinton did receive the questions to the first debate between Trump and Clinton. This hack from Russians would be utilized by the Democrats to place a stumbling block before the Trump Presidency before it even had a chance to really get started. By tripping up Donald Trump at the start of his term The Democrats could affect the chances of his team being able to get any real changes or policies to work because they would be under attack or on the defensive from the beginning. This did not work as a strategy by the Left and despite their efforts only made Trump look stronger in his resolve. The Democrats took to social media to declare Russians hacked or used the social media platform of Facebook to attack the Democrats and Hillary Clinton. Then from there they would progress to attacking Donald Trump as working with the Russians to affect the election outcome. I would like to note that President Obama once got caught on video telling Russian President Medvedev that after the election, he would have more flexibility, is the most Russian collusion I have ever witnessed since Reagan worked with Mikhail Gorbachev to end the Cold War.

Obama tells Medvedev he will have "more flexibility" after election. (Jul 30, 2015). Site name. https://www.youtube.com/watch?v=0mgQaFlo_p8

Political tactic of the Left here was effective, turn a negative about the credibility of themselves around to be a negative of the Republicans. So, this gave life to the Russian collusion investigation, which was genius from the Democrats point of view. This investigation would play out for almost the duration of the Trump administration, giving the mainstream media ample amount of negative coverage to send out to American homes by multiple outlets. The coverage was intense and extensive, and Rep Adam Schiff would brief America on events and comfort them on the fact that the evidence was plain and simple, and it was only a matter of time before it would be presented by Robert Mueller. News and every media outlet were awash with the inevitable Donald Trump guilt, and he needed to be punished for it.

The Mueller report or Report On The Investigation Into Russian Interference in the 2016 Presidential Election, was released by Attorney General Barr on April 18, 2019. The investigation would dominate all media from 2016 to 2019, almost Donald Trump's entire term and was designed to tarnish his image to the American voter. Upon its release to the public, it brought with it a sense of absolute confusion. Most American's believed that Trump would be found guilty, and that Adam Schiff had been readying everyone for the disaster of ousting a sitting President. The realization that

America had been misled, millions of dollars spent, relentless coverage, accusations leveled, and all for nothing, was impossible. Those that supported Trump all along were vindicated, got to take a deep breath of fresh air and come out from the shadow of this ugly lie. The news, talk shows, papers, radio, podcasts and everybody was talking about the Muller report and the debates would start. There still existed those that believed Donald Trump was guilty, that he should be impeached and removed from office. The very fact is, if there was proof to support that, it would most certainly have been done. The most interesting part of the Muller report is a single sentence, "it also does not exonerate him", this is interesting as it leaves America with a sense that Trump was not completely innocent. The problem is Robert Muller has not the power to exonerate Donald Trump or anyone for that matter Mueller simply does not possess that ability. Showcasing bias against Trump, he tries to save face by adding this simple but misleading sentence. Nowhere will Adam Schiff be held accountable for misleading viewers from his briefings that the evidence was so visible. The mainstream media and pundits were left scrambling to recover from constant coverage of the Russian angle. The report came out too far away from the election, that the failure to find Trump guilty would be useful to the Trump campaign and not to the Democrats. Then the shift to recover was on and the Democrats wanted to investigate the Muller report for not finding the results that would support impeachment. The Democrats were going to have their impeachment, but where would they find it? That question would be asked by many on the Republican side, "why do the Democrats and the mainstream media seem upset that their President did nothing wrong, should they not be ecstatic"? The Mueller Report did find some Russians tried to interact, but the Trump team would not respond, or work with them to conspire to commit any illegal activity and that is a win for the entire country. The findings of this report would have had the most awful lasting effects on American politics for years to come. President Nixon and the Watergate is still talked about to this day. A note should be made that Hillary Clinton was removed from working on the Watergate investigation by Jerry Zeifman, chief counsel of the House Judiciary committee. His quote says it all. He states that he did not have the power to fire Hillary but if he did, he would have. He admits he got rid of her from working on the investigation, along with a few others. Zeifman would also say, she was a liar, she was unethical, and dishonest. She had violated the constitution, the rules of the House, the rules of the committee. Zeifman would also indicate Hillary broke confidentiality rules. These are harsh words and some of these same findings could have been used to describe a few other Democrats who during the lead up to the Muller report findings being released. They conspired to mislead America, and in so doing, violated rules of the committee, rules of confidentiality, rules of ethical behavior. I would like to add that the arguments from the impeachment of Donald Trump by the Republican side, where they felt left out of the process are covered in this article by Dan Calabrese.

Dan Calabrese ——Bio and Archives--January 24, 2013. Watergate-era Judiciary chief of staff: Hillary Clinton fired for lies, unethical behavior https://canadafreepress.com/article/watergate-era-judiciary-chief-of-staff-hillary-clinton-fired-for-lies-uneth

Robert Muller would present his findings to the Senate and his responses would be less than helpful to the Democratic Party. Mueller would state he did not know the scope as an answer to Republican questions that he should have been able to answer. The investigation was his to conduct, and if there is a failure to understand the scope of any part of it, it leaves America to wonder if Robert Mueller was in charge at all, of his own investigation. The Mueller report will forever be part of the Trump administration and a black eye to the Democrat Party. A colossal failure, a colossal waste of American taxation, and purely a political strategy of the Democrats and it is completely shameful.

Chapter Four
The Divide

While there is little room for debate on the issue of the divide in the United States politically speaking, the cause of the divide is debatable between the two parties. The Left believe that the divide is due to more people being drawn either to the far Right, or to the far Left and the majority, of Americans that are aligned with the middle have gone silent. The real problem is not that people are being drawn more to the far Right, it is that people on the Left are being drawn more and more towards, far Left stances as the party policies change and adapt to more socialistic tendencies. The Right or Republican supporters have stayed true to the same values and stayed true to the same principles that the party was founded on originally. So, the divide is not that the two parties are going in two different directions, but rather, one party is going ever more Left while the other one stays the path that it has always taken. Now some might find this to be a detriment to the Republican Party for staying true to its old school values and the old principles, and some might think there is a need to change to accommodate more of our social issues facing people today. The media portrays this loyalty to values as a negative element within the Party and showcases it as a type of prejudice towards newer issues.

While there is a need to change or adapt some of the policies that both parties currently have towards social issues, this same battle has been going on forever, just the issues have changed. Over the years social issues have always played a major role in defining an era. Like in the 60's, protests at schools, universities, protesting the war, and racial equality, was something that defined the 60's. As we move into the 70's, it became more of an image issue with parents battling their sons and daughters with their changing looks of long hair, beards and the hippie movement. The 80's saw the rise of the disease Aids and the way it was initially handled by many caused an unfair stigma towards the gay community. True to nature, issues arise every era that causes a divide among voters, but never has the divide been wider than today. The widening of the divide is due directly because of social issues and issues of decency facing many Americans. The border control or the building of the wall on the southern border helping alleviate some of the illegal immigration that bolsters the chances of Americans getting jobs over employers hiring illegals to do the work cheaper. The fact that taxpayer's money goes towards funding health care for illegals when illegals, are not paying into the system or are deemed to not be qualified to receive funding from taxpayer's, is also high on the list of things causing the divide.

Another thing affecting the exodus of middle ground politics or fence sitting voters is the fact that a lot of Americans get attacked verbally for wearing Republican or Trump merchandise. YouTube videos showcasing people attacking MAGA hat wearing Trump supporters and having the media portray those supporters as hate mongers helped to create the divide. The same could be said about Republican and Trump supporters having signs in their lawn finding their signs damaged stolen on daily basis created a hostility as it was accepted to do these acts against Conservatives. As a lot of Conservatives found that they felt unsafe when it came to being able to represent the party that they support. It became an issue when out at restaurants and public events at school where Conservatives, felt attacked, or on the defensive, in a lot of instances. In fact, Hillary Clinton called for uncivil behavior towards the party that opposed what her and the Democrats felt were more important issues and Maxine Waters addressed this as well when she called for people to confront Conservatives in restaurants, gas stations and tell them they, were not wanted or welcome. The rise of this kind of behavior from the Left and the Democrat elected is a new low, as that is not what the people elected them to do. You were elected to represent the riding you ran in and the issues that those constituents face and to voice those concerns and issues in the government, not to create chaos in the streets because your side lost. This behavior is one of the worst causes of the divide because it is something childish and ethically unsound, that anyone would choose to act like this is shameful and unacceptable. When people are attacked for simply identifying with the Republican Party, democracy itself has lost. This was evident when actor, Jusse Smollett potentially created a hate crime in Chicago where he was attacked by Republican supporters, prejudiced against black and gay people put a noose around his neck, and beat him. Hollywood came to his defence, and many lashed out against Republican supporters and Republicans themselves for creating this hostility and this environment where people would do such things. After the truth came out that it was a hoax, and that two black brothers were paid to attack him and set it up for attention at the expense of a Party he does not follow, or support was sickening. Even more sickening was the lack of outrage from the Left and the Democrats for this type of behaviour, and the silence from Hollywood for such selfish and degrading acts. We see that this is not just something the Democrats and Hollywood try, teenager Nick Sandmann was attacked while protesting in Washington, he became the target of the media for simply showcasing his support of the Republican Party.

With an environment created to make one side feel uneasy, or that they are under attack for simply voting one way or the other, this is a huge failure of today's democracy. This simple act of lashing out did the most damage to erasing the voice of those moderate voters who do not align with either Party but are more issue based per election. With no safe outlet to discuss issues in public without attack or to debate the issues without attack, it caused voters to go silent on a many of the issues, while at the same time quietly aligning themselves in their own minds. The mainstream media tends to mention the divide and the cause of the divide putting most of the blame on the Republican Party or on Donald Trump himself, it is a shameful lack of journalism as the issues that caused the divide are more due to the Democrat party trying to accommodate more and more of a socialistic support group that tends to follow Bernie Sanders. Sanders had what could be considered the beginning of a third Party following, as his base was very socialistic, and young. Both the Republican and the Democrat parties were struggling to match the amount of support Bernie was gathering at his rallies. With little chance of those socialistic supporters voting for a Republican candidate The Democrats had to try and accommodate these supporters and in doing so change and adapt their policies as a Party. The funny thing about Bernie Sanders is he preaches a socialistic society which has never worked in any country anywhere in the world. And the fact that the Democrats, the Republicans and Bernie Sanders understand that it would be an economy destroying endeavor to adapt the policies of these failed countries. Bernie Sanders does not even live the socialistic lifestyle that he tries to tell Americans they need to convert to, as he has written many books creating a net worth that is on the rise with little socialistic tendencies in his spending. If he truly, believes Americans must adapt to what he says is needed, why does he not himself lead by example?

The cause of the divide and the divide itself should be a great debate subject at Universities, College, high schools and in coffee shops everywhere across America. Americans should feel safe enough to talk about issues and solutions freely without attack. Failing to do something about this hostility and failing to stand up to this kind of bullying will lead to an increased gap and cause more and more Americans to not show up and cast votes in elections. The longer that one side gets to retain this power to silence the other, the harder it will be to rectify. The more that the Media outlets get to broadcast a slanted view or create the narrative that all the problems are from the Right or Republican Party, without rebuttal, the less informed America will remain.

Chapter Five
Beliefs

The beliefs and faith of some supporters, play a major role in defining the Republican Party. This group of Republican supporters believe that a Christian based approach to many of the issues is the only answer. The Right feel that Judeo Christian values the very values that America was built on by the founding fathers are the values that we need to hold fast to, today. The Left tends to feel less convicted towards the importance of these values in politics. A great example of this would be the opening prayer of the Senate, that included a prayer to a god that represents all religions and closed with a gender neutral Amen and Awoman. Personal beliefs and faith play such a role in defining our individuality and make up so much of our daily convictions it could not play more of a major role, in how we vote. Emanuel Cleaver the Methodist Minister would defend his prayer closure saying that conservative critics, including Donald Trump Jr., had proven themselves, to be selfish, perverted by prejudice. He would go on to say his Awoman was referencing the large number of women in Congress. Showcasing the difference in loyalty to God, as there should never be any God above the Almighty, nor should we change the closure of prayer to give glory to man or woman.

Many of the issues the Democrats are taking towards policy that the Republicans have put forward tends to be an area of contention for these Christian based voters. With New York State passing laws on abortion that allow this procedure to be done late in the duration of the pregnancy, it caused a woman in the court room to stand up and yell, "may Almighty God, have mercy on the state of New York", when the bill was passed. We see many States and Governors changing to accommodate like policies on abortion. Governor Ralph Northam the Governor of Virginia has passed legislature that allows a mother and a physician to consider abortion after the birth of the child, in some instances. Leading some to argue that Northam was supporting infanticide, a claim he denies. This kind of legislature or bill opposes the Christian faith values that many Republican supporters have. Not to say that those on the Left would not be opposed to this bill, merely pointing out that many religious people feel very strongly towards this bill.

During the COVID-19 global pandemic churches were a target of many Governors in many States and people felt like there was an unnecessary restriction put on people wanting to worship. With many businesses offering curbside service or with people being allowed to go about daily life, church goers felt they should be given the option of meeting outdoors for service. In many instances churches met in the parking lot of their church and were met with police presence breaking up the Sunday service. Once back to limited numbers, members were prohibited from singing hymns. Many felt that this was a direct attack on their faith as many different groups and businesses were being allowed to function almost as normal. Once a group has taken the stance that they have been wrongly targeted or wrongly centered out it is hard to change that opinion. Faith plays such a huge role in many people's stability, or daily devotion, that it becomes incredibly powerful, to them.

Israel tends to be considered one of our greatest allies by Republicans because of our close ties with Christian values that stem from The Holy Land. The Democrats under Barack Obama showcased more of a support for Iran than for Israel when Obama and the Democrats allowed Iran a nuclear program with little inspection from American specialists. This nuclear program was one that Israeli Prime Minister Benjamin Netanyahu had adamantly objected to because Iran had called for the death of all Jews. Obama would go on to threaten to stop munitions that were supplied by the Americans to Israel if Israel did not comply with a stop building order in an area contested by Palestinians. This was seen as a stance against our Allie Israel also as a slight to Christian faith as Obama's administration was more willing to work with the terrorist supporting country of Iran. Donald Trump once in office stopped the nuclear program with Iran and sanctioned Iran for their actions and this move was so effective that it had Iran willing to talk peace with Israel just before the 2020 election. Now that Joe Biden is in office, in just days Iran has already stated that they are excited to have their nuclear program back and their sanctions removed, and we see that Iran has launched a missile towards ships being aggressive again with little to no accountability by the Biden administration. Further, White House Press Secretary Jen Psaki had no real answer to reporters when asked if Saudi Arabia and Israel were important allies to the United States of America. This after Biden was in office just over three weeks and had not yet reached out to the Israeli Leader. Trump reached out after three days, and Netanyahu has called Trump a friend of Israel, where he stated only that he had a warm conversation with Biden.

Today more so than ever it is evident that less emphasis has been put on faith more and more people are moving away from church and the value system that goes along with Christian values. A lot of times the very values that Christians hold dear are often scoffed at and used against them in many instances. Many people without asking the individual about their stance on such things as abortion, or gay marriage have been misled to believe all Christians are opposed to these things. We must remember to not assume things about others that we do not know. One element that, faith based, voters tend to require is a high level of accountability from the people they vote for. This is something that has set many politicians back when running for office. Joe Biden caught up in plagiarism scandals in past runs for President, Hillary Clinton after failing to be truthful on many happenings, like being shot at in Bosnia, or the email scandal. We will discuss accountability later, but mentioning it here highlights that, faith based, voters are less likely to vote for a repeat abuser.

The media has become overly involved with our Religious Freedoms. CNN host Chris Cuomo did a segment on his show where he discusses the lack of a need for God, that we now must just depend or lean on each other. Most media outlets portray Trump as an evil element, needing to be removed from our lives and try to align some element of Christianity, as the reason Christians should be angry. This is all done to keep people angry, and fearful, without even knowing why. The MSM, use this trick, the Democrats use policies to weaken people remaining faithful, and the Social Justice Warriors/Celebrities use Cancel Culture to silence Faith as Hate. It is every one's right to Freedom of Religion, and not up to any Left leaning element to dictate otherwise. During the second impeachment of President Trump, Eric Swalwell made a reference to God being a woman, saying, "God herself". And Bette Midler referred to the Texas winter storm, and outages of power, as God's wrath towards Republicans Ted Cruz and John Cornyn. The reference of God, or the utterance of His anger towards the Right, from a woman who has said in the past that, "religion and men are worthless", is disgraceful. The same is true of Swalwell, virtue signaling to the Left about the gender of God, only to try and appease the political demographic groups that do not even believe in God in the first place. Freedom of Speech and Freedom of Religion allow people like Bette Midler to say such things that are offensive to Christians, but she should know better. The number of A-List celebrities who join her in using offensive language towards those on the Right is growing.

Chapter Six
Programs

The programs that we watch say a lot about who we are. While programs are meant to entertain us, we align ourselves with shows that fortify either our faith and beliefs or political associations. We are witnessing a programming issue at some networks where once a star has come forward as being Conservative, their show seems to be cancelled or removed. This was very much front and center when Duck Dynasty was on the A&E network, and it was being slated for removal but due to the popularity of the show, it was not. At one point Phil Robertson was not allowed on the show or visible in any episode due to comments he made regarding sin. The comments were based on his faith or beliefs, and were his personal feelings, and experiences. Were they right or wrong? Well, that is up to someone else to decide, I am only pointing out that a movement exists where hearing a different opinion is becoming unallowed. This same situation was the cause of Tim Allen's Last Man Standing show on ABC. The show was the second highest rated show at the time it was cancelled, and ABC said it was not willing to cover production costs of a seventh season. The problem was that the cancellation came after Tim Allen, the star of the show was on some interview style shows like Jimmy Kimmel talking about being a Conservative. After Tim Allen confessed, he believes Conservatives in Hollywood are targets and outsiders, his show was cancelled. This prompted a very funny episode once his show was picked up by the Fox network where he and his onscreen wife played by Nancy Travis, are talking about a show they see is cancelled. The banter between them mocks the very situation that faced their own show and is worth watching.

Those shows that showcased family values were a real staple for networks. During the 70's shows like Good Times that presented family values and episodes centred around what it meant to have a decent moral upbringing, were highly rated. Many people growing up in the 80's spent many happy hours learning right from wrong from the Cosby Show. This hit show was a fan favorite offering fans a look inside a family that could be related to by many people. Today Bill Cosby has faced some serious claims about his personal behaviour. I mention the Cosby Show as a body of work by many great actors, that did showcase great family values. Shows like Good Times, the Cosby Show and Home Improvement offered viewers a renewed faith that moral decency was always the right choice. The shows of the 70's, 80's and 90's, were designed to be enjoyed by the entire family with little concern for content being sexual or language being foul. Many shows today are filled with Left leaning ideology and language I struggle with as a parent allowing my own children to watch. The change in programming content over the last 20 years has really taken a corner on decency and morality.

To reiterate what Tim Allen was saying during interviews on Jimmy Kimmel and other talk shows, Hollywood has become a place where Leftist ideology rules. Shows like The View are a great example of this where often a Conservative guest is invited but they are outnumbered by the hosts of the show and allowed little time to talk where they are not being talked over. The show has a hard time even being decent to the Conservative host on the panel which usually is only one person and are usually short lived before moving on to other adventures. This creates an environment where only one idea or one side of the story is allowed fair and unbiased coverage and the other is muted, interrupted and attacked relentlessly. Best example of this was when Bill O'Reilly was on and two of the hosts got up and left their own show. Barbara Walters would state that she was disappointed in the hosts that left as she said, "you never leave your own show". The reason for Whoopi and Joy walking out will be talked about later but it is fair to say that opposing ideas are just not tolerated by the Left in Hollywood.

Content pushing boundaries on today's shows being broadcast on all networks has been language, sexuality and mature content. The language people use today is much more tolerant of profanity and this is in part due to a distancing from faith as a populace and lessening of church as an important aspect of our life. This could be said also on the amount of sexuality that is present in a lot of shows. Not to say that addressing some sexuality issues is a bad thing or showcasing that sexuality issues could be unhealthy if kept silent. Blatant sexuality showcasing too much of a need or showcasing behaviors needed in order to be popular is a very damaging thing. It tends to be a very thin line between education towards sexuality and using it as a draw for the success of a show.

Likewise, many shows today have moved away from simply being sitcoms, or dramas and have moved towards being outlets for the writers to showcase their own political ideas. Risking the loss of viewership, the writers have created an environment where it builds popularity within Hollywood, but not with every-day America, and that has taken precedent over entertaining. A sharp decline in viewership of Oscar coverage and other award shows like the Golden Globes is due in part to politicising shows that have no reason to be. Changing the content from pure entertainment or comedy style writing to encompass mature content like political preference, creates less chances of the show's success. With fewer people tuning into the Oscars or Golden Globes and Hollywood staying its course on the programs it puts forward, will the need for these shows be there in a few years? Will the shows change back to entertaining once a Democrat is elected back, into the White House, and spark more interest from the everyday American again?

One of the biggest and most damaging changes to the shows we watch has been language. While I have stated already that we are moving into a time where our acceptance of profanity is much higher, we need to address it immediately. The acceptance of profanity is not just in our daily conversations, and in the language, we use at work, it is in our shows as well. Shows that are more designed for children are using much more colourful or milder profanity and it is being accepted. The use of profanity in our daily lives, like at our place of work helps to make us numb to its existence. Rarely do we go out for dinner or to any place in public and not hear people gathered using profanity loud enough for all to hear. It has become accepted behaviour to use it, and children are being permitted to speak that way at home in many instances.

Aside from language, a new trend in shows, and especially in video games has been the increase in violence. Most games are first person shooter games, and the graphics today lends to the desensitization of our youth towards killing. Many games struggle with language and violence some incorporate sexual content into it as well. I believe that empathy issues are arising from all the time our youth, and all ages for that matter, spend sitting in front of a computer or gaming system. When you couple the fact that today we are becoming less in person socially and more online/ texting socially with less empathy towards others, it creates a perfect storm. A very sharp increase in people having trouble with reality is firmly rooted in the content we allow ourselves to be inundated with.

A rise in mental health issues related to the content we allow ourselves to be flooded with directly. We are the product of what we put into our bodies. That is true with our diets, also with our programming. If we put in violence and profanity slowly over time, we will embody those elements. If that is true for adults, it is true for children as well. Children watching parents talk among friends with profanity and or finding pornographic material on computers and around the house will mimic and imitate those behaviours. This is true as well with alcohol intake, children raised in households with high levels of alcohol use, are more likely to have the same usage levels as adults. These behaviours are all part of programming, not just television, videogaming, or computer content. We program our children with our behaviours, and we showcase what is acceptable and tolerated within our households. Those behaviours mold children into the adults they become and will teach their children those same levels of acceptability and tolerance. The shows from the 70's, 80's, and 90's seemed to be highly influential towards decency and created lasting material that built up the family unit. Not to say all content today is poorly created but highlighting the fact that a change has taken place.

More content is out in the world now than ever before. With the children watching more YouTube than television shows today, the parent's job of monitoring that content is becoming harder and harder. With our busy lifestyles and some parents lack of knowledge related to the many forms of input children use today, it impacts those levels of violence, profanity, and sexual content children see. During the Grammy Award show 2021, Cardi B performed her hit song WAP, I will not state what that stands for, but it is a great example of what is written above. Cardi B performed this song on a bed with another woman, both in thongs, both being overtly sexual with each other. She ended the song with a strip show inside a glass shoe. This was performed on network television, to which children should be able to watch their favourite singers win awards. Sadly, children would have witnessed disturbing content, and someone at the network should be fired for allowing this perverted, and despicable performance from airing.

Chapter Seven
Media

Today the largest contributor to deception within our daily lives is the media. Donald Trump famous for coining the phrase "fake news" has hit the nail on the head. The term, "fake news", is ingenious as it showcases the fact that real and true journalism is dead. Once we were given the facts of situations and we were allowed, to create our own opinion without inundation of Left leaning Party views by the news outlet we watch. Sadly, today you can tell what news agency or news channel someone watches by what they say about situations that are present daily. Many media outlets showcase this type of coverage in their reporting. Repeatedly the media has been caught covering the story wrong or portraying the wrong narrative. With a majority, of Left leaning viewership, they make more money off giving them what they want. This allows them a certain amount of freedom when it comes to accountability for the content and often leaves us wondering how they get away with saying what they do. Case in point Don Lemon often rants about racial issues and has stated all 74 million people that voted for Donald Trump align themselves with the KKK.

Don Lemon: Everyone Who Voted For Trump Sided With 'The Klan,' 'Nazis,' Rioters. (Jan 14, 2021). https://www.youtube.com/watch?v=Cs8HY8Lo5wM

The media's deception in the way they dealt with and covered the story of high school student Nick Sandmann is deplorable. Nick Sandmann was a Covington high school visitor to Capitol Hill during a protest from many different groups. Sandmann was there quietly protesting when he was approached by a Native American with a drum. Nathan Phillips was that native protester, a well known, protester, he approached the teen placing the drum beside Nick's ear which is loud and, obtrusive, and was designed to achieve a certain result. Phillips was hoping for, some, kind of reaction from the teen that he could use to further his cause and somehow bolster a narrative that did not exist. The full video of the events show-cased many groups acting incredibly poorly on the Washington Capitol that day. The problem was that the media took that video and altered it so that viewers only witnessed what the media wanted the viewers to see. The media ran the narrative that a teenager in a Make America Great Again hat was responsible for the disrespect-ful actions taken place during the protests. This goes along with the negative only coverage of all things President Trump, by depicting this teenager who was quietly protesting his own convictions that day and was made to look a villain because of his association with The Republicans. The direct aftermath of this altered video gave Mr. Phillips a public forum to tell his side of the story that showcased his being discriminated upon and treated poorly by the teen. Now once the full video was showcased to the world, it in fact showed that Nick Sandmann, was one of many who were acting sensibly during the protest. Sandmann would go on to take both CNN and the Washington Post to court over defamation claims. Both would settle out of court as both were being sued for $250,000,000 each. The main problem is that the media knew Nick Sandmann was not behaving poorly or deserving of the coverage he received, but they did it anyway. The fact that a teenage life was something the media was willing to destroy showcases how far away from decency we have slipped.

Another example of the news not being truthful or using decep-tion to their advantage was to showcase a negative during a positive situation inside the Oval Office. On February 27th, 2017, during a visit to the Oval Office by leaders of historically black universities and colleges, Trump signed into power triple the funding that Obama era gave. During this visit to the Oval Office by the black leaders the media would divert attention away from the actual happenings that were going on and have their viewers enraged with the fact Kellyanne Conway had her feet on the couch. This simple trick took the attention of the viewers away from a positive and had them focus their attention on a negative situation that was not even an actual issue. Many photographs showcase Barack Obama then President, sitting with his feet on the desk in the Oval Office. If it was a respect issue with Kellyanne then it surely should have been a respect issue with Barack Obama. The media spent so much time trying to depict Donald J Trump as a racist they could not possibly showcase him giving such a huge bolstering amount to a black education fund. Despite Donald Trump's many times denouncing white supremacy and other hate groups, the media refuses to admit that he has said anything towards their denouncement. This is especially troubling when Don Lemon continues to associate Republican followers as being tolerant of the KKK and demonizes 74 million people falsely because of a narrative that the media portrays about Donald Trump.

The media has a love affair with the Left, as it has showcased with Hillary Clinton, allowing Hillary the questions to the debate back in 2016 with Donald Trump. Recently, the media use, weak questions when asking Joe Biden anything. Joe Biden was the centre of a sexual allegation by miss Tara Reade, to which even Kamala Harris agreed she believed the victim. The media refused to ask Joe Biden about this sexual allegation and gave him a free pass multiple times when it should have been one of the strongest pressed issues by journalists trying to get to the bottom of the allegation. The questions put towards the White House during Trump's administration were ridiculous in nature, like if Trump was sorry that the South had lost the Civil War. Many questions by Jim Acosta, were designed in nature to get a certain level of frustration from the Press Secretary, or the President himself. As before noted during Trump's administration the coverage from news agencies like CNN, and MSNBC, were 93% negative towards Republican actions. This love affair is not going anywhere as CNN's April Ryan suggested that journalists should not expose Biden's contradictions back in December of 2020. While other reporters are saying they will cover the Biden administration differently than that of the Trump administration.

The greatest example of the media being deceptive is the coverage that Chris Cuomo received when he had COVID-19. Daily briefings from Cuomo's basement were given and even his brother Governor Cuomo would state how poorly Chris looked in appearance. Chris would talk about the difficulties of dealing with COVID-19 and how hard it was to not be with his family. It seems that Chris Cuomo was not isolated in his basement but was across town with his family at the new home they were building and got into a confrontation with a passer by who noticed he was not at home isolating at all. Chris would admit to getting into this altercation but no accountability for his misleading America to believe he was in his basement away from his family. The deception would be further portrayed as he had a reveal live on air coming out of his basement to his awaiting family. Hypocritical of him, after admitting he was across town with his family at their new home. The real problem was that Chris Cuomo was willing to put builders and his family in jeopardy of contacting COVID-19, and all the while pretending he was taking necessary precautions.

Further proof that the media is in fact an extension of the Democrat party is very evident in that 2 1/2 years the mainstream media broadcasted very damaging coverage of the Russian collusion, without proof. Many networks ran storylines and had guests on that would speak to the fact the Muller report would turn up evidence that Donald J Trump colluded with the Russians. This tactic by the mainstream media of covering the Muller Report on a constant feed from an angle that had already found guilt was building support behind a Democrat party that had not yet selected a candidate for 2020. After 2 1/2 years of covering the Muller investigation the mainstream media had to report that there was no evidence to support any real collusion.

The most damning to the credibility of the mainstream media and strengthening of claims they are fake was the coverage of rioting and looting as mostly peaceful, during the lead up to the 2020 election. Even while video coverage of fires raged through businesses and neighborhoods, while looters stole from stores the mainstream media narrated that the protesters were mostly peaceful. Very evident to the viewers was the fact that destruction and chaos raged in the wake of these protests. Also evident was that the media was giving this anarchy a free pass. We truly have turned a corner on decency when the media covering the actions of individuals that are causing destruction and chaos are willing to candy coat those actions to protect Leftist ideology. Joe Biden was asked to denounce the actions during these riots and protests, and he responded by saying that he was not in power, which would have lent some persuasion of other leaders to call for these actions to stop. During the capital riot where Trump supporters stormed the Capitol building Joe Biden called on Donald Trump to act swiftly on denouncing their actions, a simple act he himself would not do swiftly, and only once he was pressured relentlessly.

In order to truly find unity and solve some of the issues presently facing America the media is going to have to face more stringent and strict guidelines on their coverage. If the media is given the option of altering what we are seeing designed to enrage viewers on issues but not be enraged on the exact same issue by the opposite Party, there must be some fallout. Today we are witnessing many confrontations between people at work or at home, based solely on things the media tells you to be angry about but when pressed on what the actual issue is, are unable to give the details. Many con-frontations starting with allegations of racism toward President Trump have ended when the person accusing is unable to give a single example of when he said anything racist.

The ownership of the main media groups, and lesser networks, is where the first steps need to be taken to ensure we are being given the truth on subjects. Our daily news should not be mixed with the beliefs or values of a political party or by an owner who leans one way or the other. When it comes to making money off the news, at one time the side that got the "scoop" got the lions share of coverage and the prestige of breaking the story. It seems today that the side that can make the story's narrative fit the picture or storyline they are selling to viewers gets the free pass. CNN President, Jeff Zucker said in an interview by Vanity Fair back in November 2018 that Trump dominates, and if they shift away from Trump, the viewers would, dwindle. This creates a certain amount of power for the media giant, as they have a Left leaning viewership, so they simply put a Leftist style slant on all things, and the viewership is happy. Sadly though, the actual truth gets lost in the storyline, and we are fed misinformation. Same could be said for FoxNews who have a Right leaning viewership base. Erasing the bias is impossible, lessening it to create a more uniform or fact-based presentation is the goal that should be the finish line for all. Now I admit even this book is not written without bias, as I myself am a Christian Conservative, but decency is not owned by only one Party, nor should it be the goal of only one Party.

Deception used to create negative attention towards Republicans was very evident in March while the entire world was starting to deal with a Global pandemic, the media was more set on games. Kellyanne Conway giving a press update, was pressed by Yamiche Alcindor of PBS about the term, "Kung Flu", and asked if it was an offensive term to the White House. Kellyanne would go on to say it was, and that Yamiche should use the time and platform to oust the Republican that she was referring to that used the term. As she was pressured to give an answer, Yamiche tried to say that she needed to protect sources and that is how it works. Kellyanne would pressure her more saying she just needed to give the name of the Republican and the entire world would know who it is, and they could stop talking about hypothetical situations. Yamiche would press Kellyanne about how Asians are feeling and if she cared about how Asians felt. To which Kellyanne finally tells Yamiche that her husband is

George Conway who is himself half Filipino, making her children twenty-five percent Asian, subject dropped. The Mainstream Media, and the Left continue to use, "gotcha" style questions when covering the Right, and without knowledge of Conway's connection of Asian heritage, decided to use the wrong attack.

It is important to note, in today's world we talk an awful lot about hypothetical situations, like Trump being a racist, but having no actual instance of him saying racist things. We are then moved to conversations and arguments under this misguided approach, which will only ever amount to endless nonsense. As a reminder, when discussing politics or religion try to not get sucked into conversations that are based on "what if's or I think", over the facts of any situation. And if you do not know the facts, please be adult enough to admit you know nothing about a situation but will research it and be ready another time to discuss it.

MSNBC anchor Brian Williams was suspended without pay for falsely stating his helicopter came under fire in Iraq back in 2015, which was a move designed to create honesty in reporting. But as Hillary Clinton would go on to state she landed in Bosnia under sniper fire that turned out to be false, it seems as if the Left are able to say anything without account. The media was held to a higher standard at one point, but with Don Lemon and Chris Cuomo being allowed to say the most insulting comments without account is CNN's failure, showcased by money over truth, and that true journalism is dead.

On election night 2016, Van Jones called the win for the Trump team a "White lashing", alluding to the fact that the winning side was against Black lives. Don Lemon and Van Jones both black men, report from a perspective that all things Right are racist. It takes away from actual situations of racism ever being reported by these men. It allows those people of either side a chance to sidestep accountability by stating that ALL things are racist with Republican supporters. Much like the use of comparison to Hitler for Donald Trump. It washes away the importance of remembering the atrocities, it down-plays, the historical horrors for political gain, and it diminishes the lives of the men that fought in WWII to stop the maniacal Adolf Hitler and the German Reich. We should expect more from our News, and the people that report it.

Deception is a powerful tool, and when used to mislead a group of people it is ugly. Case in point the "cages" that Donald Trump used at the southern border. Over the four years that Trump was in the White House, the media giants along with the Democrats would depict the use of detention housing as cages to make it appear evil. During debates for the 2020 election Trump would ask Biden "who built the cages Joe?" Biden would not answer this question and of course it was Obama and Biden who built them. Now that Biden is in the White House, we see the media has given the "cages" a new more friendly name. Not only have they renamed them but refuse to talk about the immigration crisis that is facing the southern border, with an endless flow of people trying to get into the country. A shift from a hard prison like encampment, to a friendly care giving facility under the Biden administration.

Chapter Eight
Players

In today's world of politics, the main players from each Party really are representation of what the Party stands for. The main players from each Party also showcase the character of the Party. You are either doing a justice to the Party or an injustice depending on your actions. When you hold public office, you should be held to the highest account, and when your decisions and the policies, and laws, that you create affect millions of people your intentions should be true, and the accountability should be high. This is where many of the main players on the Left have showcased incredibly poor judgment, and incredibly poor behavior in any kind of unity with the Trump Presidency. So ironic is it that now President Biden is in office, the Democrats are calling for unity and all things they refused to do themselves. Over the course of Trump's four years, the main players from the Democrat side have really showcased that they are willing to use safeguards in the American political system as tactics against a President for nothing more than a power grab. This poor behavior was not saved for just President Donald J Trump but for all those associated with him like Judge Kavanaugh and Judge Amy Coney Barrett. To truly look at how the main players misbehaved you would have to look at the situations specifically to highlight those times where they let us down. This chapter will highlight some of those times and some of those behaviors to which those people should be held accountable.

Starting with speaker Nancy Pelosi and her interview where she so happily and blissfully gloated about the fact that President Donald J Trump was impeached, as if it was a personal goal. Nancy Pelosi during Trump's State of the Union address had pre-torn her copy of his speech so that she could at the end of his speaking, tear them in half, symbolizing her disdain. The childish behavior from someone that holds a prestigious position as speaker of the house is baffling as we have not witnessed the likes before. Nancy is no stranger to getting herself in hot water as she endorsed a, stay at home order during the pandemic, also issued a mask mandate, supporting the closure of small businesses. Now during this mandate to wear masks and closing of businesses Nancy needed a haircut, she was caught on video by store owner without a mask and attending a closed business. The video was released to the public and Nancy decided she deserved an apology from the store owner. Delusional to the fact everyone else had to suffer her decisions. This kind of behavior showcases a lack of reality by Mrs. Pelosi and adds to the double standard that exists between the Left, and the Right. Back in March of 2020 when President Trump started putting in place procedures to limit Americans from traveling around and spreading the COVID-19 pandemic, Nancy Pelosi took to the media to tell Americans to get out and do the opposite of Trump's orders. This unprofessional and unethical move put American's health directly in jeopardy all to oppose orders and hope to make the opposition look bad. This same move was done by Democrat mayors like De Blasio, and the mayor of New Orleans, followed by Senators from New York all telling Americans to get out ride the subway, "we are a hardy bunch". With a new push to impeach President Trump a second time Nancy Pelosi is leading the way in her own words to directly affect Donald J Trump from ever running for President again. This is not the intended use of impeachment.

Rep Adam Schiff shares the same geographic area and State as Nancy Pelosi also shares in the decisions that have led to an increased number of homeless living under plastic on the streets in San Francisco. Aside from policy issues that have allowed this to take place, Adam Schiff's behavior related to the impeachment of Donald Trump and the Muller report is where Schiff's accountability is lacking. When relating to Americans on an almost daily basis about the ongoing investigation by Robert Muller into President Donald Trump and Russian interference in the 2016 election Adam Schiff would allude there was guilt evident. On his briefings he would openly state that it was only a matter of time relating to what he himself witnessed as evidence and reported to the world that Donald J Trump was guilty. Schiff more than once stated he saw enough evidence of guilt. When the Mueller report was finally released to the American people and everyone could celebrate that the President had not done anything wrong, there should have been a Senate Judiciary committee meeting set for Schiff to answer for those briefings. However, this behavior was not called to account and Adam Schiff continued to act the same way without any answering for misleading Americans for the duration of 2 1/2 years. Which led to Adam Schiff having direct actions in the impeachment of Donald Trump. This first impeachment would be highlighted by witnesses not being allowed to answer questions or for rebuttal and would see Republicans not invited to meetings related to the procedures. Once the impeachment hit the Senate floor Adam Schiff was wanting to conduct more of this style of proceedings. After Trump was acquitted of impeachment again Adam Schiff should have faced accountability for his behavior to which nothing happened. What this allowed was a two and a half year, long investigation into President Trump's behavior that clearly had no evidence from day one. It also allowed the Democrats to utilize the mainstream media to tarnish the image and character of a sitting United States President. For these actions Adam Schiff should not be allowed to hold office as it clearly was a political tactic to tarnish the Republicans and not used for its original intent because there was not enough evidence or grounds for the investigation or impeachment in the beginning.

Moving on to Alexandria Ocasio Cortez and her fellow squad members. AOC as she is also known is an advocate for green energy which is admirable except for the way she conducts herself in advocating for it. It is not her Green New Deal that AOC should be ashamed of, but her behaviour towards fellow elected members. Her act of visiting the "cages" during Trump's Presidency, and lack of any interest in them now that Biden is President calls for questioning. If she was so moved to pose for doubled over in grief, pictures of the mistreatment, and subsequent housing of detainees, she should be incredibly more moved over current numbers. Only now AOC has become tolerant of the border situation under Biden's Presidency, highlighting a lack of real concern for the people, using them as pawns for political gain. Where is her visit with film crews in tow to talk about the devastation now that the situation has intensified hundreds of times over? AOC's account of the happening during the Capital Riot also calls into question her character, as she insists, she was almost murdered, and that she was in danger in her office. Her office is in a building across the street from where the riots were occupying.

Rashida Tlaib has openly called for sanctions against Israel, herself being of Palestinian heritage, and openly advocates to have Israel punished while never condemning actions from the Palestinian side. The Israeli/Palestinian tensions are not one sided, and personal stances by sitting members of the American government, should not be trying to create more tension for the either side. Recently she has come out and stated that Israel is a racist state based on the global pandemic vaccine rollout in Israel. Tlaib insists that Israel, one of the most vaccinated countries in the world is denying people like her grandmother access to vaccines. However, Palestine has not reached out to Israel for help, and is also responsible for their own healthcare of residents in Gaza/West Bank, according to the Oslo Accords. Hamas governing of the West Bank and Gaza Strip has forced Israel and Egypt to place a blockade upon them. Creating a logistical challenge in getting vaccines to them. Understanding that Tlaib has family and ties to the Palestine side, and a concern for her family there, is commendable. What is not commendable is her continued insistence that Israel be boycotted and sanctioned without noting the tensions and struggles towards peace in the region is a shared responsibility. Tlaib should also call on fellow Muslim countries like Jordan and Egypt to help the Palestinian people, not just declare Israel the responsibility due to the contested and heated nature of the two sides.

United Nations Peacemaker. (13/09/1993). https://peacemaker.un.org/israelopt-osloaccord93

Rashida has also tried to stir up controversy using the mainstream media when she wanted to go visit her elderly grandmother in Palestine after openly calling for sanctions against Israel. She would stir up controversy and then ask for permission to enter the country. She was denied access to Israel upon first asking because of the comments that she made in the media. Which is the result she wanted to further advocate her disdain for the Jewish state. Once Israel found out she wanted to visit her elderly grandmother she was immediately allowed access to which she declined acceptance. If members of the Democrat party are tolerant of this type of behavior clearly anti-Semitic and are tolerant of the hatred in the statements Rashida Tlaib openly shares with multiple media outlets, it is a disgrace. The Democrats have called for Donald Trump to denounce hatred, and White Supremacy countless times, and even though he has many times, the media refuses to give him the credit of doing so. Sadly, when the hatred and prejudice is within their own Party, the Democrats are silent, and will not call for Tlaib to denounce her hatred. Together the Mainstream Media and Democrats would promote the image that Republicans support hate under Trump's leadership against Black American's, they refuse to address actual, real hatred that is born and spread right inside their own Party by Squad members. Ilhan Omar another member of the Squad shares Tlaib's view of Israel. Her description of events on Sept 11 where "some people did things", is a disgrace, and the Party should want to hold this behaviour accountable. To openly call for Unity, and accountability from Republicans, but silently allow racial issues to fester among themselves is indeed a double standard between Left and Right. Where is Van Jones, or Don Lemon, where is the leadership of the Democrat Party, or Joe Biden on these issues? Too busy calling all 74 million Trump voters racist to see that true and real racism is alive and well inside the Democratic Party.

Maxine Waters after Trump won the election in 2016 openly called for supporters to approach Republicans and supporters to harass them. "Tell them they're not wanted here anymore", she called for uncivil behaviour towards the winners of the American election. How can this be tolerated? How can a sitting member of government be allowed to issue such hatred and divisiveness, without accountability? Maxine Waters also took to the streets to tell protesters to be more confrontational, and to stay out longer, demonstrating incredibly poor behaviour, bordering on grounds to be removed from office in my opinion. Well, it happens far too often in the State of California, and Pelosi, Schiff, and Waters are the front runners.

We witnessed two appointees to the Supreme Court under Trump's administration. Judge Kavanaugh and Judge Amy Coney Barrett. Two respected and deserving people with stellar professional track records, representing the values worthy of SCOTUS status. Before being confirmed to the SCOTUS Judge Kavanaugh would be subject to accusations of sexual misbehaviour from Dr. Christine Blasey Ford, from the early 80's. While the events remembered by Dr. Ford came up with little evidence, and a lack of anyone who could remember attending this party, there was only her account of the events to back her accusations, along with a passed polygraph test. There was, however, numerous women who believed her accounts of the attack as she describes it, and they took to the streets to protest Kavanaugh's appointment. It is not my job to decide if either of them, are telling the truth or lying, however, if you decide to wait until someone is at the threshold of achievement, and offer no tangible proof, it will look like an attempt to deceive. Ford choosing to wait decades to come forward left room for doubt, and increased chances of error in the accounting of the events. I offer no opinion towards Ford or Kavanaugh. The reason I mention this situation is to highlight not Dr. Ford or Kavanaugh but the large number of women who came out to oppose the appointment. Yet at the same exact time as the Kavanaugh meetings, Democrat Keith Ellison, was facing sexual and physical abuse allegations by his ex-girlfriend Karen Monahan and her son. Monahan had zero backing from the women opposing Kavanaugh, and actress Alysa Milano, who was present daily at the Kavanaugh meetings. Why was Monahan not given the same support and protests?

Joe Biden was accused of sexual misbehaviour as well by Tara Reade, during the 2020 election. This was met with little support for Reade, and the Mainstream media had multiple interviews with Biden before they even managed to ask him about it. Kamala Harris stated she believes Reade's allegations, and has not mentioned it since being named Biden's VP pick. If you believe Biden to be an abuser of women's rights and freedoms, why would you align yourself, a woman with him? And why the double standard, one for Kavanaugh, and Trump, yet another for Ellison, and Biden? Harris was vocal in the Kavanaugh case, yet remains silent on Biden, Ellison, and Governor Cuomo, during their allegations. The point is not who is right or who is guilty, but there should be a standard that both sides are called to, facing accountability equal of one another.

Before we get to the Republican side of the players field, we could not and must not leave out the Clinton family. I would like to say, that during the Reagan, Bush, and Bush2.0 eras policies could be debated, but integrity could not be questioned. I will give that same statement to Barack Obama, as I was not a fan of any of his policies, but he brought no disrespect to the White House or the office of the President of the United States. If ever given the opportunity to discuss his poor choices of policies, I would jump at the chance.

The Clinton's. A name that brings forward so much debatable material. Starting with Bill Clinton, and his impeachment trial over his actions with then intern Monica Lewinski. Not only did Bill take advantage of this young woman, who had obtained the incredible position of White House intern, he disgraced the Office of POTUS. Adding to this affair behind his wife's back, he would have another affair with Gennifer Flowers. Bill Clinton behaviour while in office was not fitting of a President, and it leaves one to question how the Left has not banned him from attending any Democrat functions. Outside of the sexual nature of the Presidential term that Clinton served, he was effective in his job, but that does nothing to lessen the fact he has damaged his reputation. And if others are being called to answer for actions of yesterday, why is Bill not called to answer for his? There are also claims from other women of alleged misconduct, and payments of settlement. If those are true or not it still leaves one to wonder with such allegations and history how Bill could be sought after by Vice President Harris to help with women's empowerment? Harris appeared at an event put on by Howard University, her alumni, with Clinton which created an outcry of anger due to his reputation. Why then do Democrats continue to call for others to face the music but continue to embrace Bill Clinton?

Hillary Rodham Clinton. Well, this woman takes the cake as far as behaviour that should eliminate you from ever running for POTUS. If Trump can be impeached after being out of office, in order to negate his chances of ever running again, Hillary should be barred as well. Her actions towards inflating the "not my President" behaviour, and the failure to concede the election after calling Trump out saying he would not do so, cements her from ever being POTUS. These actions created clearly destructive behaviour for the duration of Trump's Presidency. Starting way back at the Watergate trials, where she was found to be unprofessional, she has arguably remained so. She used humour to hide her criminal behaviour of allowing sensitive material to be sent over unsecured devices, she used her position to misinform America of the actual cause of the Benghazi attacks. She has lied about snipers firing at her, she has lied about the potential danger towards her daughter during 9/11. Hillary continues to put forward an image of unbelievability. The last real straw to break so to speak was when she went into the first debate with Donald Trump, and she had received the questions, showcasing a lack of integrity towards fairness and decency. There is no excuse for accepting those questions, and no excuse for misleading people to avoid answering for one's actions.

Donald J Trump 45th President of the United States of America, is a very charismatic man. He has had some very public battles with women like Rosie O'Donnell and is not afraid to voice his opinions. On his television show The Apprentice he did not hold back on people coming to the boardroom, or when he fired them. He has stayed true to his personality before, during and now after his term as President. What you see is what you get, but he kept his word on his promises, and accomplished a tremendous amount in four years, surpassing that of almost any other previous President. Trump did not shy away from questions, nor did he only answer pre-approved questions. His Presidency was full of combative questioning from reporters and his aggressive answering. A much different approach than that of Biden's and being more open and willing to engage reporters.

Trump's Presidency was a very defining period in his life, giving his Presidential salary away to charity, and embracing strong stances on policies that created enormous chances for job creation. His unemployment levels were lowest in history and the people loved him that followed the GOP. Now was Donald J Trump Presidential? Was his way of attacking his enemies like Pelosi or Hillary justified? Well, that is for each person to decide for themselves, and maybe evaluate based on how he was attacked himself by those he attacked. The fact remains, Donald J Trump had the best first term Presidency is recent history, based on doing the opposite of Barack Obama, and will be further highlighted by Joe Biden going back to all things Obama. Having Trump's term in office bookended by Obama and Biden will cement his administrations greatest achievements, as the successes they were.

Other leading Republicans, like Mitch McConnell, Jim Jordan, Dan Crenshaw, Lindsey Graham, and Rand Paul, were quietly and tirelessly working to combat Democrat games, while not being involved in poor behaviour themselves. This is what true character looks like and needs to be stated. Vice President Mike Pence was a soft spoken, presence during his four-year term, and showcased true class in his behaviour. The fact that Trump was the only real target of the Left, MSM, and Democrats alike is a real testament to the Republican Party, Senate and House elected GOP.

Now there are some Democrats that deserve to be mentioned here as being honourable. The reason I do not mention them is because of their silence on calling out the behaviour of so many in their own Party, they lose my respect. Case in point the non declaring of the genocide of the Uyghur's in China, the Biden administration is unwilling to declare it for what it is. Fear of retaliation or ostracizing from within the Party has silenced those Democrats that should be appalled by the actions of fellow Democrats. The lack of voices appalled by the riots, the actions of Maxine Waters, Clintons, Swalwell, and others. Some secondary players, behind the scenes on both sides have had their actions questioned, but my referencing those Democrats that behaved improperly are elected officials, and I feel should be held accountable. From their behaviour in public and for their use of social media to further promote their behaviour.

Chapter Nine
Social Media

Today we are very much controlled by social media. If you need to verify that, look no further than the recent banning of President Trump by Twitter. The problem is not that Donald Trump is banned, the problem is Twitter chooses to ban conservative voices and conservative groups, all the while allowing hate groups and leaders of terrorist organisations to use their platform. An example of this would be the Ayatollah of Iran being allowed to tweet, but Donald Trump is not. Social media has become such a large part of our daily lives that we allow it to control how we get our news. Many people draw on shared information across many different social media platforms as the main place for their daily information. This is a terrible place to draw your news from as it is often presented without any accountability for false statements. Social media memes are usually shared between like minded people, from sources that align with the person sharing the meme's own views politically or religiously. Social media like Twitter and Facebook being allowed to control who is permitted to share information with the masses is frightening. By silencing conservative viewpoints and or allowing free speech for Left leaning people, and organizations only it infringes on freedom of speech.

In today's busy lifestyles we rely on others to do most of our heavy lifting when it comes to the news and politics. Clicking onto our social media to check in with our friends and get our hourly update coupled with information on the world around us is addicting. The simplicity it offers is far easier then taking the time to go to a specific website and read the news for ourselves. The biggest problem with this platform is the quality or accuracy of the information being shared. Often the information shared is not accurate and is heavily bias one way or the other. This allows many Canadian and Americans to be filled with false information and misleading information ready to debate these situations at work or in the coffee shop. What people should start doing is looking into those things that they see on social media and verifying them with an actual news source before taking on others that are informed. Back to the censorship that these major social media platform giant's control, they Fact Check or put a notice under Donald Trump's tweets but do not under Left leaning posts. By allowing this censorship and this amount of power to Twitter and Facebook, they can silence a President because they do not support that Party is frightening. Social media has become one of the most important tools in an election cycle, having a strong social media presence is key to winning many younger voters. The single greatest way to reach this demographic is through social media and if one Party is allowed use of the platform uninterrupted and without account it allows a significant advantage to that Party.

A very striking difference between how news was once shared and how it is shared today is the creation of the meme. More and more people are relying on memes as their main source of forming opinions politically. While many memes are funny and creative the problem again is the reliability of the information they are presenting. If you couple the fact that one side can share information without regard or fact checked, it gives the false, illusion that their information is correct. By simply putting the Fact Check notification on the bottom of every Donald Trump tweet it called into question the reliability of the source. More and more Republicans are facing this same scrutiny while hate groups and the Left are not. Often memes will be shared across more than one platform and emailed back and forth to coworkers and friends and sadly, this is where the majority are getting their information today.

One of the most difficult things facing political parties today is how to counteract false information from being shared and damaging material sent out. This is the problem with social media platforms, it creates a thriving environment for that. You can comment but often comments on social media take on a life of their own, and often because typed responses are open for people to form the context in which the reply was meant, the original message gets skewed. With such heavy use of social media, the fact that we are becoming less and less social when we are face to face, and in fact rely more on our social media accounts to present ourselves, is a sad reality. Many people choose to text instead of call friends, or group chats will be set up through text and social media accounts where people will interact, without any real connection. With this environment some people have found a place to come out of their shell, or for personal entertainment use this platform to attack others. Most people who do not possess the confidence to talk to people about politics or religion face to face will use their social media platform to relay their feelings. Now this is fine, if people remember to be respectful and empathetic towards others and their feelings. Sadly, most of the time, this is not what happens, people will take to the platform to attack others and it has created an entirely new place for bullying.

The bullying that takes place on social media is not reserved for just high school kids, or public school but for all ages and all users. At the school level children will use the platform to create situations for other children where they are picked on or centred out. This has had some devastating results as the suicide numbers skyrocket. Another trend where social media is losing the battle on decency is the amount of sexually explicit pictures being shared. Some young women are pressured into taking exposed pictures of themselves and sharing it and find if they do not comply are the centre of attack. However, once they do share the revealing pictures they are often used as a bullying technique and these teens lose either way. If married couples want to use their Facebook or other social media platforms to share pictures with one another, in an attempt, to keep fires lit I am supportive. But the excessive reach that this platform has on the youth and the bullying that goes with it I am not sure we are better off today. The youth are not the only ones affected by bullying on social media. Today with the cancel culture we are finding many people are losing their jobs based on tweets or posts, that they put on their personal profiles. Adults need to remember that often social media platforms, are a reflection, of who we are and if we are a reflection, of what we do for a living there is a cross-over area that we are accountable for. Since Joe Biden has taken office some in the media and in Hollywood have taken to Twitter to lash out at the Donald Trump's administration. Unfortunately, what was shared was not accurate nor was it ethically sound. Bette Midler, Tim Matheson, Peter Fonda, have all taken to social media to lash out at the Trump family. Sadly, Peter Fonda decided to attack Barron Trump, who is an adolescent this is ridiculous behavior for an adult. Bette Midler and Tim Matheson both attacked Melania Trump on her English. English is not Melania Trump's first language and many in Hollywood have associated her poor English with not being as intelligent as some of the wives on the Left. Never have I witnessed anyone being attacked for knowing more than one language and being called unintelligent due to the proficiency of all languages they know. These Hollywood celebrities have allowed their political view to showcase a lack of decency they have towards the treatment of others. Social media was also a major player in the Nick Sandmann fiasco where the media portrayed the teen misleadingly. Some in Hollywood attacked the teen for simply being there protesting his convictions and getting caught up in the agenda of a media giant. When these posts go out, they are simply deleted when there is any kind of backlash seldom, do we see and apologetic post on a follow up. The same could be said during the Jussie Smollett ordeal where once it was revealed that he might have arranged his attack, little was done to take back the accusations posted by many in Hollywood. Seldom do we see where people are held accountable for their tweets or posts but sometimes it happens. It is problematic when only on a rare occasion is accountability found. With the cancel culture some people are being called on posts that are not offensive in nature but are somehow being made to look the part. I will get more into that in the chapter cancel culture.

I think the best thing that parents can do for their children is monitor the social media platforms that they are using and check in once in awhile to see what conversations are taking place there. Something that adults should remember to do is to keep their private life off their social media especially their work happenings to avoid any kind of conflict of interest. Many people today will post very personal things or a viewpoint on politics but not want any kind of response back which is ridiculous. If you post something expect a reply especially from those that oppose what you posted. Making sure that any kind of interaction on Facebook, Twitter, Snapchat is kept mature and without attack, remembering that the people responding to you are your friends so keep things decent.

Chapter Ten
Accountability

This chapter is going to be dedicated to accountability and I feel that accountability is something that we are lacking across the board today. I feel that many on the Left are getting a free pass when it comes to answering for the things that they say. Currently we are witnessing President Joe Biden make statements about the COVID-19 pandemic that are contradictory to his platform when he ran against Donald Trump. On the lead up to the 2020 election Joe Biden made statements that he would deal with the pandemic, and they were going to end the pandemic. In his first 2 weeks in office Joe Biden has come out and said they cannot change the trajectory of the Covid19 pandemic. The problem is not that Joe Biden made promises that he will not be able to keep during an election, the problem is that the media is not calling him on this lack of delivering the promise. Herein lies the entire problem one side gets a pass where the other side is held to a much higher account. False statements from either side or from teacher's, religious leaders, bosses, coworkers should all be treated the same, making false statements should be held accountable. False statements should not be something that we become used to or numb to based on your principles or political party. The things that we choose to say especially towards others should be something we take the time to ensure is accurate, empathetic, respectable, and truthful in nature. And if your behaviour is called into account, like this book is doing for many on the Left, it should be something based on actual circumstances.

One great example of not being held accountable for false statements would be none other than Elizabeth Warren. Elizabeth Warren has for many years now claimed Native American heritage. This is something that ended up becoming a battle between Donald Trump and herself. Elizabeth Warren claimed to be native on her law license and was using it during campaigns claiming to be a minority. However, once she did a DNA test it came back that she was 1/1024 Native American. That means if she is 1% of any other ethnicity, she is more than she is Native American. The media should have done more to call Warren on her statements and pressed her more about admitting she is minimally Native American. Claiming this status Elizabeth Warren is misleading people and trying to gain an advantage by saying she is a minority. A few years ago, any politician making openly false statements would have been asked to resign from office, those politicians openly making false statements would not have been allowed to run at the end of their term if they did not resign. This is in fact why Joe Biden did not get elected President of the United States in his previous attempts. During those previous attempts Joe Biden was caught plagiarizing other people's speeches and using them as his own without giving credit to the original speechwriters. Joe Biden also said he graduated at the top of his class with three degrees when in fact he only graduated with one degree and was nowhere near the top of his class. These kinds of statements may seem small or petty, but they are a direct reflection of the character of the person making the statement.

Kamala Harris has been caught in quite a few statements that may be untrue, and we see today she is now the Vice President of the United States. Kamala has stated that she does in fact smoke pot because she is Jamaican, something her own father has stated is disturbing. Her bragging about using a substance she imprisoned so many for using is completely lacking in accountability. She is also part of the team that is removing people from working at the White House who have admitted to past pot use. Kamala would go on to say she listened to Biggie and Tupac when she was in school, but she is too old to have been listening to them in the time frame she gave. More recently Kamala Harris has gone on record telling a story of how while she was a young child, she was an activist and how she fell out of a stroller and was fussing afterward which prompted someone to ask her what she wanted and she says, "fweedom". The story is very compelling and paints her in a great light where she looks to be from the beginning of her childhood interested in civil rights. The problem with the story is it mimics exactly a story Martin Luther King was famous for telling. The stories are so similar that both stories use the word freedom pronounced incorrectly by a child. If you showcase falsehoods about yourself, be it your heritage, number of degrees you earned, where you placed in your class, or claiming other's stories as your own, you should be held to account.

Another moment where accountability should have been at the forefront is when Judge Kavanaugh was being accused of sexual misconduct by Dr Blasey Ford. During the same time however Democrat Keith Ellison was not held to the same standard when he was being accused by his ex-girlfriend, and her son. The main difference between the two cases was the amount of proof that was present against Ellison, 911 calls, hospital records and pictures, yet there were no protests no Senate hearings and no accountability. We see that this same pattern is present with Joe Biden's accuser being believed by Kamala Harris but after Harris was chosen to be Biden's running mate there is no longer any talk of her belief in the accusations. Donald Trump was accused buy ex-porn star Stormy Daniels of paying her hush money and the media were adamant they would find Trump guilty somehow. After months of running the story and making a superstar of Daniels lawyer Michael Avenatti, Daniels was ordered to pay $300,000 in damages to Trump. So why the difference between Donald Trump and Joe Biden, why do we see one side being harassed and the other given a free pass by the press and the media with barely a mention of the accusation? If the media does not hold The Democrat members of government accountable for their actions but report endlessly about The Republican side

and their behavior it represents hypocritical double standards. Both
Parties need to be held accountable by their own Party, the media,
and the voters in order to ensure that decency remains at the forefront of those in power positions and law creators. The laws and
ethics that elected officials must follow pertaining to their actions,
behaviors, and statements they make should be far more adhered to
and enforced as the behavior is quite visibly out of control.

Joe Biden has a box of files pertaining to his behaviours, and
interactions with other World Leaders locked away in the University
of Delaware, away from the voting public until he is done public
service. How is this possible? Should the public not know the very
dealings that their President is capable of, or has done already in the
47 years or more in public office? If the box of files is in fact pertaining to his dealings, that means they happened as a representative
of the people, they should be aware of the dealings. Donald Trump
would never be permitted this same blessing, in fact Trump's tax
returns, and his business dealings have been a matter of court actions
until his term ended as President. So again, one side is allowed to
hide his past while the other is having his personal life dragged into
the spotlight, where is the same level of accountability?

When you think about the Clinton family, you do not associate them with accountability for their actions. While Bill never
really saw any accounting for his actions of false statements to the
American people about his sexual behaviour with Ms. Lewinski, or
his many other women, he should have been impeached. Recently
Bill has fallen from grace in the public eye, and people are concerned about his involvement with VP Harris on women's empowerment. Hillary has never really had to account for her behaviours
either. Starting all the way back to the Watergate Investigation, her
description of events at Benghazi, and the email scandal. Hillary
would however not be held back by her previous behaviour, and in
fact go on to showcase many of these same traits in many different roles. Her handling of questions about the Benghazi attack, her
smashing devices instead of turning them over to investigators, and
her unethically obtaining the questions to a Presidential debate. All

these actions should have been held to account by far more people or at the very least her fellow Party members who bare the guilt with her for not speaking out in protest to them. The voters were the first ones to hold her to account during the 2016 election, and Hillary would be caught off guard by it. Refusing to take responsibility for her actions, or accepting the outcome of 2016, continues to demonstrate behaviour needing further account.

Which leads me to her fellow Party members. All of whom seem to support the actions of rioters and looters over the course of the last year. Not once did we hear from Joe Biden, Elisabeth Warren, Nancy Pelosi, Chuck Schumer, Adam Schiff, or Kamala Harris speaking out for a call to stop these actions. Nor did we hear from countless Democrats in either the Senate or House for that matter, for a call to have leaders denounce the actions of rioters. In fact, Biden seemed to help the people doing the rioting as his team members donated to their bail. With none of the main players calling for these riots to end, but in fact lending some support behind them. Calling them "mostly peaceful", a statement echoed by the Mainstream Media networks, only strengthened their actions. A fact that was not lost on the 74 million Trump voters in the 2020 election. A call from the Left like Maxine Waters, and Hillary Clinton for their supporters to be uncivil until the White House is again belonging to a Democrat President is absurd. These actions were direct causes in creating a divide, then the very people that called on the behaviour, demonized Trump as the cause. Great political tactic by the Left, but where is the media pointing this out, where is the journalists that make a living reporting the happenings of Washington? Well, it appears as if they are only an extension of the Democrat Party themselves, and the silence is frightening. Kamala Harris shared a link to help pay for rioters to be bailed out, which resulted in one man getting out only to assault someone and be arrested again.

To further showcase this MSM and Democrat union, we look no further that the Russian collusion that was the center of a, two and a half year, long character assassination on Donald Trump. With Democrats like Adam Schiff using the media to broadcast his predictions based on actual proof he witnessed, supposedly. In the end however, the Mueller Report came back vindicating Trump of any wrong. How can the media and the Democrats make so many statements of guilt, broadcast so much on one subject without any proof, and in the end just walk away without even a single word of apology for the slander?

There are a lot more instances that could make the list of times where accountability was lacking between the MSM and Democrats. When a State and City openly promotes open borders but put into place special clauses to protect them from prosecution, they are admitting to their failures. San Francisco is the places, Kate Steinle the victim, murdered by an illegal immigrant Jose Ines Garcia Zarate. Now the sanctuary State of California, and the sanctuary city of San Francisco can not be sued by victims of illegals as per the laws created to protect them from such actions. So why did they feel it necessary to create these laws of prevention if they truly feel being a sanctuary is in fact safest for the people? Well, the answer is they do not think it is safer and created the laws to protect themselves from being held accountable once the inevitable happened. The tragedy is that Kate Steinle lost her wonder young life, her family lost their beautiful daughter, and hopes of a future family she would create. By withholding information from ICE, the State and City are both partially responsible for her death, as the killer is in fact a repeat felon from Mexico and has been deported multiple time before.

The media is the most disappointing aspect here. The way they openly cover the Left in a flattering way, while demonizing the Right highlights the death of actual journalism. Gone are the days where reporters tracked a story down, and broke the news, now they just pitch softball questions and help answer them for Biden and his team, after asking the most leading and damning questions of the Trump team. If any real change is to come about, if we are going to be accurately informed, we must first call on our Mainstream Media to be accountable for the broadcasting they do, and the content and context of their coverage.

Another area where influence and accountability, needs to be more kept in check is how teachers and professors interact with students. Having a very Liberal teacher or University Professor use their political preferences to instruct students, and or allow it to be less accepting of conservative minded students needs to be stopped immediately. One professor at Marshall University in West Virginia, "wished Trump supporters get Covid19 and die" before election day. She made these remarks during a Zoom meeting with her class. Trump had stated he would defund schools that did not correct this kind of behaviour, and he is right, it needs to be held to much higher account.

Perhaps the greatest example of zero accountability on the side of the Democrats is Eric Swalwell. Swalwell who sits on the United States House Permanent Select Committee on Intelligence has been associated with suspected Chinese spy Christine Fang or Fang Fang. The real problem is that a breach by a foreign country allowed one of their spies to infiltrate the political dealings of the United States, should you still qualify to sit on an intelligence committee? Well, the answer is very clearly, no, and true to the nature of the Left, Swalwell is not owning this as his fault, he is blaming Donald Trump because he opposed Trump. Again, sidestepping any responsibility for their actions. Without a doubt, Eric Swalwell is a threat to the intelligence of the United States and should be made to be accountable.

With the border crisis becoming more evident daily, the influx of immigrants will have to be accounted for in the close future. Not only are these people unmasked during a Global Pandemic, but are untested, unvetted and are seen as potential votes for the Biden team. Refusing to acknowledge the crisis, and with the want to abolish ICE or any deportation of felons from the USA, the Democrats are creating a high potential for more violence within its borders. At some point, Biden will have to account for the inevitable happening, the question is, who will he blame for it?

The border crisis is out of control in only two months time from when Joe Biden became officially the President. Yet, no talk of the crisis, no labelling it a crisis, and no visits to the border by either Biden or Harris. When asked about visiting the border, Harris laughed it off. The very facility that the Democrats called cages and depicted Trump as evil for using are full to overflowing capacity under Biden, and yet no concern from the Democrats who not long ago were sick about the facility being used.

Chapter Eleven
Hollywood

Once Upon a time, Hollywood and the people making movies were so highly respected, they called that era the Golden Age of movies. Today we are witnessing a far different Hollywood and the fall from grace is legendary. Harvey Weinstein being sent to jail for his sexual behavior spanning numerous years is just a start. Even though many young actresses struggled with Weinstein's behavior, actresses like Meryl Streep would refer to him as God during award shows. This allowed Harvey to continue his actions as his fellow actors and actresses turned a blind eye. Thankfully in the end the truth prevailed, and some accountability will come of it.

Today's celebrities like to throw their political views around quite heavily. Robert De Niro after Donald Trump won the election in 2016 went on record during an interview saying, "I'd like to punch him in the face". Madonna stated she had thought an awful lot about blowing up the White House, and once offered to perform oral sex on anyone willing to vote for Hillary Clinton. Madonna made the remarks at Madison Square Garden and went on to further entice people by saying she was good and was not a tool she took her time. This speaks to where we are today in regard of decency, when we allow such disrespect to hide behind either comedy our celebrity status. The remarks showcase a complete lack of decency and have no place in the political sphere. Anyone making such comments should be ashamed of themselves and need to reflect on themselves inwardly. Madonna is not the only celebrity to showcase how low they can go. Kathy Griffin did a photo shoot with a severed bloody head that resembled Donald Trump. This photo shoot was celebrated among the Left but when an outcry from decent Americans produced a backlash for Griffin, she tried turning it around saying that Trump had gotten to her, and it is what he wanted to happen. After some time had passed, and Kathy Griffin having once said she was sorry, eventually would return to the photo shoot and claim that she was not sorry after all. Jussie Smollett is a great example of Hollywood's lack of decency, and lack of self respect. His claim of a racist homophobic attack that happened late at night in Chicago by his apartment designed to depict Republican voters in the most awful and negative way was nothing short of evil. He claimed he was attacked, a noose was put around his neck, a substance thrown on him, and he was verbally assaulted for being gay and black. Only details that he could remember were the assailants were white males in MAGA hats that attacked him for being gay and black. Now the support that he received initially from his peers in Hollywood was commendable. However, the attack that his peers did on Republican supporters was not, and there would be no apologies after. Once investigated and the truth brought forward that the attack was potentially, self planned, and paid for by the actor, designed for his own attention at the expense of conservative minded Americans is almost unforgivable. Have we really reached a point that Hollywood celebrities afraid that their character on a popular show might have run its course, that the only thing they can think to do is plan a hate crime? Now true, one actor does not represent the entire actor's field in Hollywood, but we are still waiting for apologies from numerous celebs on the Jussie and Nick Sandmann issues. Being outspoken is fine, being wrong requires an apology.

Some actors in Hollywood have come forward stating that being openly conservative hinders the ability to get work. Gina Carano was fired from Disney's The Mandalorian for statements about how the hatred can be used and how it is present today in Hollywood. The Democrat Party and the supporters of the Democrats in

Hollywood who claim the Party stands for unity and fairness to all, prohibit work to those fellow actors that support Republicans. This hypocritical stance showcases Hollywood in our current era. Perhaps the greatest realization among American voters is this hypocritical stance showcased in the lack of viewer support for award shows like the Oscars. The Oscars should have been far more watched as we were in a global pandemic and more and more Americans were at home able to tune in. The content of the award show is perhaps part of the reason as it has become more of a political platform then a show designed to showcase the movies and shows themselves. More and more often we are witnessing the politicizing of those things that are designed to be entertainment based. From kneeling during the national anthem, to award shows making hosts yell slogans, everyday Americans are being bombarded with one sided political, views. Not to say there is no room for either side to use their plat-form to promote much needed change, only highlighting the fact to which it is done and how it can take away from your intended meaning. During elections it is easy to sway voters in a negative way, away from the intended message with the wrong approach, there is a fine line.

Alyssa Milano further highlighted the hypocrisy of Hollywood when she was so outspoken about the appointment of Brent Kavanaugh to the Supreme Court. Milano would attend the daily Senate meetings and was outspoken before and after the proceed-ings about how women's rights needed to be more protected. Alyssa Milano was more concerned about the way in which Kavanaugh politically was supportive, than she was about the situation at hand. The more pressing issue for Milano was the future decisions being made on abortion issues and if that meant keeping Brent Kavanaugh from sitting on the SCOTUS then that was what was needed, even at the expense of a man's name, family, and career. Where the hypocrisy came into play was Alyssa Milano was stating she supported women's rights but failed to be outspoken when it came to Democrat Keith Ellison, Joe Biden, or Governor Cuomo facing the exact same allegations. If women's rights were Milano's true reason for protesting and not her willing to destroy a man's life for her political views, she would have been equally disturbed by all three men's treatment of women. Neither Ellison nor Biden would face any real pressure or questioning about their behaviour, while Kavanaugh took to the Senate meetings to defend his name, and his record. A note should be made here that Amy Coney Barrett faced similar attack styled questioning even being asked by Democrat Senator Mazie Hirono if she has ever sexually assaulted anyone. Making this line of questioning or the accusations of sexual misconduct look more strategy based and could be more of an issue of libel.

Shows like The View, and Real Time with Bill Maher, are often designed to promote the Liberal ideology. This is made very evident on most episodes by inviting a single Conservative minded guest and using numerous Liberal minded guests/hosts to question them. This is also true of the panel itself on The View, where Meghan McCain is the only Conservative outnumbered by four Liberals. On McCain's return to the show after maternity leave, Joy Behar told her she did not miss her when she was gone. CNN and MSNBC also use this style of attack to quiet the Conservative guest as most times in all these examples Conservative guests will not be permitted to speak uninterrupted. If these shows want to create an environment where ideas can be shared or talked and debated equally and fairly, the panel should be equal and fair. CNN has a habit of losing the feed of Conservative guests that are doing a great job of defending their position, and right in the middle of their point, the feed is lost. This tactic is not lost on anyone, and only makes you look less prepared for the debate.

I would like to state that not all of Hollywood is to be painted with the same brush and should not be lumped into the same category as Madonna or Joy Behar. Mark Wahlberg once said actors should not talk politics as they are out of touch with everyday Americans. Tim Allen understands this mindset as well, as his popular show was dropped by ABC before being picked up by the Fox network.

Something to remember is that we are all allowed a single vote, and we are all allowed to have our own opinions. These differences are what the art of debate is all about. Having many different views on many different subjects by many different people is the best way to share and learn, we must embrace that, not look to ways to silence it. With many in the celebrity world showcasing a lack of patience or tolerance for opposing ideas, followed by the Democrats and the Left faithful, people are allowing other ideas to be silenced. People following this mindset bring that mindset with them into their private lives, work environments and other areas of their lives.

Chapter Twelve
The Workplace

Starting off this chapter we must understand that unless you work in a place that is political in nature, politics should remain outside of work. If on your breaks, and or during conversations with coworkers, politics comes up, remember to be respectable in your comments. Nowhere is there room for name calling, or the use of profane language, it only makes you look immature.

The workplace is somewhere that the Left is targeting today with the use of misinformation. Through mainstream media outlets, the Left uses misinformation to enrage their viewers in hopes that they will in fact share their distain, including fellow workers. Confrontations over this misinformation are often heated when met by those fellow workers that are more informed. One such example would be arguments based on Donald Trump being racist, where the media would have you believe Trump is in support of the KKK, and unwilling to denounce them, when in fact he has done so many times.

Remembering that other people do not share every idea or belief you do is important. Starting from a place of respect and remaining there even if the other person is not willing to do so, is a great way to keep a conversation from escalading out of control. You can argue about non work, related ideas, but if it creates a riff or divide it will affect your job performance. Being careful to avoid conversations that you realize maybe designed to make yourself or others offended could end poorly for you. There are also those people out there that want to use people's political or religious beliefs against them and will start conversations only to ambush them.

Today we see great changes within our daily lives and the workplace is no different. Today's workplaces are more open to other people's feelings, gender identity and self image. We must remember to never use these areas as punch lines in jokes, because jokes are not funny if we hurt someone in the telling of a joke. A lot of these areas are new to older workers, and some people maybe have personal issue with changes, but that is not a legitimate reason for hurtful behaviour.

A good chance of being taken to the Human Resource Department of your workplace is to be openly offensive towards others and you will not find tolerance in these areas. Some changes are coming about due to the change in our societal beliefs changing, and our religious beliefs becoming less prevalent. Even if your religious views of some social challenges facing others differs remembering to keep those views to yourself and respecting others is of the utmost importance.

Pronouns we use to describe ourselves or our gender can be a place of argument. Jordan Peterson the Toronto Professor who rose to fame for refusing to use pronouns regarding gender, speaks to this. His take on the subject, is you must be willing to be offensive in order to have dialog. Peterson also feels that under the Liberal Government in Canada, Justin Trudeau has gone to far by legislating what words we can and can not use. His finding, it infringes on our Freedom of Expression. That maybe true to a degree, however, we must be knowledgeable enough in the art of conversation, that we can express ideas without the offense towards others identity.

Within some Unionized workplaces politics can play a major role. Unions and their Presidents will often persuade brothers and sisters of the local to throw their support behind a single Party and tolerance towards differentiating from that is not met with much acceptance. This environment can not be tolerated, and openminded personal decisions must be left to the individual. In some instances, a Union will hold a vote to allow input into which Party will receive the public support from the Union. This is a great and very diplomatic way of giving the members their say. If it is not taken advantage of or low numbers turn out for this process, it is squarely on the union members for not embracing the opportunity. To each, and every Union President that allows the process of a fair open vote to unfold on their watch, all that can be said is, great job.

Unfortunately, there is inside some workplaces an aspect of silence the opposition. This is a cancer that must be cut out and removed immediately. If there is only tolerance for like minded individuals in your career, you are sadly closeminded and creating an environment of regression not growth. When we do not allow an opposing idea to be presented or heard, we create an environment around ourselves that only tells us what we want to hear. This is never the best way to form an opinion or make decisions to move into the future on a positive note. We must embrace those differences, and allow them to either justify our idea, or change ideas to become successful.

Two companies that have faced backlash from the Left recently are Chic-fil-A and Goya Beans. These companies are the best example of how a statement can be used to discredit or destroy and silence an opposing idea. Political views of both companies made them targets of the Democrat faithful and calls to have the companies shut down were alarming. These companies employ large numbers of people, and the cry to shut them down would have hurt many families, but through blind hate and inability to hear an opposing idea, the big picture became less important. Thankfully, they did not get shut down, and this tactic of cancel culture did not work.

Chapter Thirteen
Cancel Culture

The single greatest threat to democracy is the Cancel Culture, and how it silences those ideas it deems to be offensive. The problem is they deem any and every idea, or opinion from the Right as offensive. The goal is to allow only those of likeminded views to have freedom of speech, while all others need to be silenced. Gone are the days where you can debate ideas or discuss among friends and coworkers the differences you have, on many subjects. Having a conversation on racial issues, or political issues in public can encounter a cancel culture person, and the fall out is usually intense.

Cancel Culture is designed to feed fear into people on the Right, silencing them from having equal right to speak their minds. All while those on the Left are given freedom to say the most absurd things without any mention, like Madonna claiming she would blow up the White House. Another example of this at work is when Hairstylist Jordan Hunt kicked Marie-Claire Bissonnette during an abortion protest in Toronto, Canada. Hunt and Bissonnette differed on their opinion and while discussing their differences, Hunt planted himself, stuck out his tongue and kicked Bissonnette in the shoulder, sending her phone she was recording the event on flying. Hunt would take off running, but police would use the video evidence to arrest him later. Both sides were out protesting that day, both sides have their valid points, but only one side was allowed their opinion. Two major things that are showcased by this action is a) violence is deemed tolerant when used against Conservatives and b) male violence towards women is tolerant if that woman is Conservative. In this situation, no one from Hunt's side stopped him after his attack, and held him accountable for his violent attack on a woman. These kinds of incidents appear throughout Canada and the United States sadly, and work towards silencing people through fear. The very side that claims to be more tolerant, and more supportive of women's issues fail miserably to showcase that claim through their actions.

The trend of not being able to hear an opposing idea leads to more troubling behaviour. As in many cases, if that idea is from someone in a position of authority, the call then comes to remove them. It becomes the culture of the Left to remove all things different and tolerance is only for what the Left agrees with. We can not go through life having every opposing idea or view shut down and removed from our lives. If that happens, we remain in a bubble unable to function if told, "no". Similar, to a small child throwing a temper tantrum in the grocery store over a box of cookies, if you give that child what they want they will learn to keep doing this every time for a desired result. So true is the Cancel Culture, if it is not stood up to, it will be allowed to receive its desired result as well.

Perhaps the best illustration of this behaviour is the removal of President Donald Trump from social media platforms like Twitter. By allowing Iran's leaders to call for death to Israel, but not allowing the President to use the platform it showcases the need for more accountability towards these platforms. By silencing the leader of the Conservative side, and many other accounts that are Right leaning, these social media giants highlight the bias present. With social media becoming the biggest election tool a candidate uses, Right Wing candidates, risk being shut out by these giants, allowing a large advantage to one side. Removing tweets or Facebook posts that the administrators deem to be offensive, silences one side, as the guidelines, for the offense is set by those supportive of the Cancel Culture.

This culture has also crept into our daily lives at work as well. In some instances, people have been taken to the Human Resource department over conversations regarding religion or politics. While I have stated already in this book these subjects should remain outside of the work environment, they do tend to come up periodically. It is not that they come up, it is when someone wishes to remove your voice from the workplace due to it being different that the problem occurs.

The Democratic Party has often used the premise that they are the Party of tolerance, and unity. This is not what we witness from this Party, and that is very evident. Calling for uncivil behaviour without accounting for the chaos it brought and using Cancel Culture to remove anyone that is opposed to their policies is not tolerant. With the Democrat side using the Mueller report attempting to remove Trump from office, then wanting to impeach Trump on the findings anyway, is a clear example of that intolerance. Continuing to further try to remove Trump from office by using a call to Ukraine, then Maxine Waters even making references of impeaching Vice President Mike Pence to remove both from office. This is not what the American people want the government to be working on, and yet Trump's administration still had the best first term Presidency of any President in the last thirty years.

The Cancel Culture placement of racist or hate label is what the largest fear is. Through the Mainstream Media and social media, the Democrats were able to create an image of a racist, xenophobic, leader in Donald Trump. No matter how many times Trump denounced the KKK, by refusing to broadcast that aspect, they created a call to remove him based on it. Taking video footage and changing it to support their narrative, even after being caught, remained steadfast to that claim. This video evidence would be presented at Trump's second impeachment hearing. Many arguments were waged on this narrative and won on the premise of "tell me one time Trump said anything racist". His push for a southern border wall was deemed racist, and his claim that illegals had to be returned to the countries they belong to. The twisting of statements, and the inability to hear from the other side of the spectrum creates a den of tension. This is not reserved for just the Republican President it is used against the

Conservative masses as well. Once in awhile the Left will get caught up in their own web, but not enough, it needs to end, it is a cancer that will eventually destroy more than just the Right. Once it has successfully silenced any opposition, it will then turn on itself and silence those within the Left that go against the majority. This has already happened in life a few times, like Nazis Germany in 1939 to 1945. It only came to an end with the loss of millions of lives and incredible sacrifice.

Stopping this culture is a huge job, it involves people standing together, it involves people learning when and where to voice themselves and learning who to talk around and who not to talk around. Freedom of speech is a civil liberty we all share, when one side tries to infringe on that, there must be push back, there must be a stance taken.

Donald Trump as President put a travel ban on countries he deemed to be of concern to the safety of the United States. Shortly after Joe Biden became President a reporter asked Biden's Press Secretary Jen Psaki about this ban. As Biden lifted some bans then put some back on. Psaki stated that the previous administration put a Muslim ban where Biden was banning the country. It is these kinds of tricks and twisting of reality that leads to the masses being misinformed, and we see an inability to for the Left to hear opposing information. Trump was treated terribly by the media and Democrats alike for using the "cages" to house children at the southern border, but Biden built them and is using them at a 700% capacity during his border crisis. Where is the media or AOC, where is the outcry from those groups that labelled Trump, where is the Celebrities calling for humanitarian rights? Silent, because that type of labelling is reserved for the Right only.

The supporters of the Left have over the course of 2019 and 2020 gone on a rampage removing historical figures from the American soil. Removing the Confederate Flag from government buildings and any Civil War Confederate statues as well. Lumped into the category of Cancel Culture is President Washington and Jefferson, as both were slave owners. Christopher Columbus was also attacked, and a push was put forward to change the name of Columbus Ohio to Flavortown, in support of chef Guy Fieri. With over twenty-five thousand signatures to back this desire.

True to fashion the Cancel Culture would not stop without going after someone that is remembered for achieving great things for his country. This is what happened when the Left went after Abraham Lincoln. In San Francisco, the High School named after Lincoln was deemed to be not allowable, by a 6 to 1 vote. Why you ask would Lincoln's name be removed, it was deemed to be offensive, in their minds, that he did not believe black lives mattered, and his treatment of the Indigenous. The very man who took on the Presidency of the United States of America and was entrenched into battle to free slaves and be the Emancipation Proclamation creator. This Proclamation freed 3.5 to 4 million slaves and made them forever free of their slavery. To further showcase the senselessness of this, cancel culture, the Emancipation Memorial in Lincoln Park Washington, which was paid for by emancipated slaves earning wages of their own, needed a fence to protect it. Democrat Eleanor Holmes Norton plans to introduce legislation to remove the memorial. If Abraham Lincoln was not for the betterment of Black lives, and acted to free them of the confines of slavery, who is safe from this Cancel Culture agenda?

Democrat Veronica Escobar from Texas is using Cancel Culture, and fear to silence critics of Biden's border crisis. She has attacked Gov. Greg Abbott and his statement about migrants having Covid19 and allowing it to spread under the circumstances present at the border. Escobar has called his statement racist and is hoping to use the word to silence anyone from talking about the border situation instead of calling on Biden to fix the situation. Sadly, this is a common tactic of the Left, and labelling people as racist should be reserved for those actually being racist. Escobar claims that the word, "surge" is military like and therefore, is somehow racist. Allowing only a single voice, or viewpoint and using power of the government to entrap those citizens, is the very formula of socialism. The Left and many of Biden's policies are leaning towards socialistic tendencies, and they need to be opposed, not allowed free reign.

Chapter Fourteen
Socialism Mindset

Socialism has gained a huge following over the last few years, and the amount, of younger voters that are flocking to the ideology is alarming. Bernie Sanders is the largest voice in the socialism advancement with a huge following. Sanders call for a more socialistic approach to the problems of today while ignoring the facts of socialism all together, is a concern.

"Hoarding all the wealth", is a common phrase heard amongst the younger voters wanting to start life out without any debt or labour towards their own success. This phrase is the embodiment of laziness, and the promotion of theft. Demanding someone else with financial success give their money to those without is wrong, and it kills entrepreneurship. It is not that these young voices are opposed to having wealth, but rather are unwilling to work towards their own success, instead demanding a portion of someone else's.

Free education is a great concept, and it works great in places like Israel, but it also comes with a loss of other free services, as there is only so much money in the budget. Those students that want to further themselves and attend University or College taking courses designed to create a life after school should be given more help. However, making education free would have to attach guidelines and parameters to alleviate time wasting or career student situations. President Joe Biden is being pressured to cancel over one trillion in student loan debt, which would stop the incentive to look for work.

By taking away the student debt, the person now has no pressing matter to get them motivated.

When young adults graduate from College and University they are in debt. Depending on the school chosen to attend, with some Ivy League schools costing more, a diploma or degree from these schools brings a certain amount of notoriety. Those students that graduate in debt work hard to create opportunities for themselves to gain well paying jobs. The goal set to pay off the debt and move up in the company to become successful is illustrated daily by watching the top executives drive fancy cars, dress nice and have homes in nice areas of town. This environment is where capitalism creates chances and builds dreams of success. That young adult starts to create chances for themselves, then after moving up in the company starts to lessen their debt and move into a better position, they can save some money, or buy a nice car, dress nicer, feel the excitement of success.

If a young adult is hired with the lack of debt, and expectations of success given to them, that company will eventually fail. If on day one the junior employee expects the top executives to give a portion of their hard work to them, and that the lifestyle gained through that hard work also be given, what does that build? It builds a lazy, poor work ethic worker who expects the lions share to be done without any labour to themselves. This is not the formula for success rather the recipe for disaster. Universities and Colleges should be made to keep the cost of education lower, with increases not being inflated so that only a select few can attend.

Dinesh D'Souza encountered this socialistic mindset on one of his university tours. A young male student stood up to confront D'Souza on his Conservative platform and advocated for society to give back to those that can not afford to attend better schools. His stance was that of stolen wealth through slavery and other sources and wanted education to be handed out to less fortunate students. The problem is with free services there is still a cost, and someone must pay that tab. It is either that the school itself, or tax-payers money needs to be used to pay for those attending. This point was made crystal clear when D'Souza focused on this young man and his admittance that his position of attending that school was a state of privilege. D'Souza would ask the young man if he was willing to give up his enrollment for a less fortunate person to take his place. This was met with excuses and an unwillingness to do so. Highlighted by D'Souza telling him if he is not willing to follow his convictions and to do first what he demands others do with their "so called" privilege, he is in fact a hypocrite. Instructing the man to first do what he feels others should do, then and only then will people be willing to follow.

To be wanting of others to share or to contribute to your success you must be willing to do the same when you are asked. This is where Bernie Sanders fails to follow his own advice, and just like the young man Dinesh D'Souza confronted, Sanders does not first give of himself. Bernie Sanders advocates for Venezuela like socialism, even after the economy failed, Bernie continues to advocate for it. Socialism has failed in every attempt in every country applied. Bernie uses the socialism ideology to sell books and to keep a position in government where he has created a net worth of millions. Now under his own advice, he should be giving this to less fortunate people of his community, but he does not. Sanders and his wife enjoy multiple homes and a lifestyle nowhere close to that of which they preach. Once asked and confronted about his wealth and the hypocritical lifestyle the Sanders lead, Bernie responded by telling them to write successful books if they wish to live as he does. This returns us to D'Souza and his comments, if you are not willing to do what you ask of others how do you expect anyone to follow you?

Bernie Sanders once said it was a good thing to stand in line for bread, this is the single most insane statement he has made. Showcasing that for Bernie, he has found a permanent niche where he can sell books and keep a paycheque coming in, without any real threat to his lifestyle. Being held accountable is not something we see the Left doing to their own, so Bernie Sanders is getting that same free pass on his hypocrisy. When Hillary Clinton used the DNC to work against Bernie, and secure the Democrat nomination for the 2016 election, Bernie put up a weak fight for fairness. Then in the 2020 election the DNC again realized that if Bernie were to win the Democrat candidacy, his platform would be incredibly damaging to Democrats in the House and Senate. Bernie Sanders should know that if elected his policies would in fact destroy America and is happy to continue filling rallies and selling books to create himself a luxury lifestyle while advocating American youth demand free passes to success.

To cover the cost of education and health care in the United States for everyone, it would bankrupt the country. To take from the "wealth hoarders", of the USA, it would not pay for the education let alone both education and healthcare. The simple math of it being unattainable is lost on a generation who base more on feelings than facts. Not just lost on them, but the prominent people like Sanders, University Professors, Teachers, and quite frankly adults that call for this form of theft of wealth, to still come up short of covering costs. Life is hard, unfair, and offers no guarantees, but hard work and dedication usually offers some gains. At the very least, it creates a sense of gratification, and achievement for those things you worked hard to obtain.

We are killing the spirit of success, the spirit of enterprise, and accomplishment. When we give a trophy for first place and for last place where is the desire to better ourselves? If you put in zero effort but attain the same, result as the person who trained and practices until they become the best, what would change your effort going forward? The answer is nothing, and the same goes for the person in first place, why would you try and work hard to be the same as last place. This is not what builds a country, company or person into better versions of itself. Seeing a person who worked hard the last twenty years to build a great lifestyle for their family should be a milestone you set for yourself. While today's socialistic mindset followers see that success as something, they demand a portion of, and deem it unfair. The entitlement is beyond words.

Often, the Scandinavian system of socialism, in Norway, is talked about as a perfect example of what we need here in the West. After a look into the policies of how it works, it would be difficult to obtain that here. The single greatest difference being the tax rate to personal taxes. A tax rate of 45.9% creates a huge burden as it is the same rate for middle and low income, families. The benefits of social income for senior citizens, is commendable but it does not address the effects it would have on those lower income families, daily lives. The wealthy in both Canada and the United States would find wealth havens for their net worth to prevent paying this taxation. The effects to small businesses, and to the disposable income of families would be catastrophic. Without disposable income, new cars, clothing, travel, services like massages would be crippled by the taxation. The disposable income from each household would be turned into income for other households.

Chapter Fifteen
Entitlement

If the Democrat Party is guilty of being entitled, how then can we blame the followers of this Party for being the same way? After the 2016 election and the cries from many Democrats like Hillary Clinton and Maxine Waters to be uncivil came forward. Those cries showcased that the Democrat Party did not care that the electoral voters had in fact wanted a Trump administration, they only cared about the power of the White House for themselves. This entitlement was the focus of many attacks on Donald Trump over the course of his entire Presidency. They started with allegations by an adult movie actress, and a lawyer in Michael Avenatti. Avenatti would become an overnight success getting famed coverage from most mainstream media and Hollywood shows like The View. The Mueller Report was an attempt at destroying Trump and his ability to work effectively as President, in hopes that he would fail miserably. Then the impeachment not just aimed at Trump but calls from Maxine Waters aimed at Mike Pence as well, further showcased it was all about power from the Democrats.

The behaviour was not lost on the Party faithful, like the media. The media used its position to cover Trump and his administration in a negative only light, even if great things were accomplished, they never reported them. The best example being Kellyanne Conway's feet on the couch instead of reporting the education bolstering bill being signed into power at the desk. So, what is deterring the new generation from being entitled? Well, the problem is that it is not generational at all but speaks more to the individual person. Saying that it is generational is painting everyone with the same brush, and it is unfair, and wrong. Entitlement is something that needs to be combatted as an idea not a new generation issue.

This entitlement has given us a new YouTube sensation, called "Karen". Most people enjoy watching people freak out over situations where they feel they can act out or say anything they want. In reality, there are consequences for such actions. Gone it seems are the days when people demanded respect by being respectable. We have witnessed an increase in demand by people to have their opinion allowed while not respecting others back. Confrontations between people based on entitlement might be entertaining to watch on YouTube but showcases a lack of mental health in our society, or ability to cope with daily situations. We have become a covetous nation, and people, who want others, belongings, power, lifestyle, work, and money. The Bible tells us in the Ten Commandments not to covet, as we move further away from the church being important in our lives, we are less likely to see where we fail God's requests of our behaviours.

The workplace might be the single greatest increase in entitlement issues. Not just from new employees feeling entitled towards the lifestyle that senior executives are living but expectations across many different occupations. If senior employees have worked 30 years for a better schedule more holidays and preferred days off, it comes from an expense of years of service. Often, new employees will demand the same treatment as senior employees claiming they do the same job. The wages are the same just some of the perks go to senior employees. In unionized shops, seniority plays a key role in many of these situations and an increase in complaints from newer employees in situations designed to ensure senior workers remain working are usually disputed. Forgetting that one day those junior employees will become the senior employees, efforts to eradicate those perks will come back to haunt them if successful.

Entitlement is a scary thing it causes us to act in ways we do not put forward our best selves. It causes us to become violent in some cases, and sadly we see on many occasions, adults acting very poorly in front of their children. When we teach our children to behave like this, or if we demand special treatment for our children at either school, or sports, we are teaching them to become entitled. Once this lesson has taken root, it is almost impossible to root out, or change. Demanding other people's money or possessions is theft and becoming violent in those demands is why there exists law and order.

I return to the Democrat Party behaviour after the 2016 election loss, if there were more accountability for the actions taken, and the accusations met with more severe outcome, it would change faster. Rep. Rashida Tlaib often uses social media and her platform of position to speak what many say is Anti-Semitic rhetoric about the State of Israel, this should be met with harsh results. If both sides were expected to uphold the same level of accountability, we would not see the level of entitlement the Left feels they possess.

We have become a people that has put ourselves first and put those around us beneath our wants and desires. We need to get back to a less selfish mindset, and revisit that Commandment, thou shall not covet. Those voices calling for Socialistic policies and for others to give of their success for an easier path to success for themselves is the greatest example of entitlement. We have become so covetous in our journey through life that we view those things that should be examples used to drive our ambitions, as demands for equality. Unless we receive a portion from those who have already obtained success, we declare it wealth hoarding and privilege, and demand it through protest. This is something learned from the Bible story of Cain and Abel. Cain killed his brother over envy and jealousy, today we are still witnessing this same trend. The lessons learned in the Bible are less known today, as we move further away from a more religious based family structure to a more worldly based structure.

Chapter Sixteen
Family Structure

Today the family structure looks differently than it did thirty years ago. Today we are more accepting of lifestyles other than the typical male/female parenting format. With acceptance of this change to what we used to define "family" as, we have opened a world of growth.

Mainstream Hollywood shows broadcast the new family structure and help alleviate the pressure to conform to what once was the only structure accepted. This broadens out into social media and helps further strengthen the mental health of those dealing with many different issues like how to dress, or what gender they prefer. It is our job to ensure acceptance and we should only be intolerant of those people purposely inflicting hurt onto others. Mental Health is everyone's job.

Despite whom makes up your family structure, be it two males or two females or male/female, a value system is still necessary. Growing up in any era, the value system was reinforced not just through parenting but through television shows and school teachings. The same is true today, the need for a strong value system has not changed or gone away. The value system, however, is going through a change as society is moving further away from religious beliefs, we once held more esteemed. We are also witnessing more entitlement and it is affecting the value system as well. Revisiting the change in profane language talked about earlier in this book, acceptable amounts of profanity by parents today has changed severely. Each household is ultimately responsible for setting the acceptable language, shows allowed and the behaviours we are witnessing are going through the greatest changes to those levels.

Many households are changing the use of gender terms, and even forgoing placing any label of either, on children all together. In some cases, the parents will not identify as either gender themselves. In rare cases we see an effort to show children that men can be women and women can be men, parents will dress opposite to show acceptance. While some people find this to be drastic or abuse even, we must remember that setting value systems is up to each household. It is when the value system set by people are thrust upon others, we see conflict.

Gender has become such a subject of importance over the course of the last ten years. We see that parents are sometimes jumping on board forcing the issue on small children. This is where it goes beyond setting value systems of your household. Parents looking to be heavily involved in the movement, will sometimes advocate that their small child is transgender. We have seen in the past where parents place a pink square and a blue square on the floor and have their child crawl to the square that they identify with. The problem with this premise is, small children are not aware of the colour associated with each gender, and the best out of three will always be won by the first one that gets the biggest cheer from parents. If the child goes to a blue square and the parents wanted the pink the reaction will be less intense. Once that child realizes a more positive response is gotten by the pink, it will return to the pink more often.

Who is parenting our children the parents or technology? Well, the answer is according to your schedule. Today we are more reliant on technology for everything, and parenting is no different. After a long, day of work, it is difficult to come home and engage children sometimes, and this is where most people are guilty of wanting a few minutes of wind down time first. That is not problematic, what is however, is when families are sitting at the supper table, and everyone has their phones in hand distracted by technology. Often parents today are under more pressure and demands making it difficult to go home and not continue to work. With this distraction a drift away from forming close bonds goes without notice until it is too late.

Parents from eras back like the 80's and 90's would often reprimand, or scold children of the neighbourhood in heartfelt concern for the safety of the children. Fast forward to today's society where it has become more isolated and less likely to approach or say anything to other children out of fear of attack from their parents. This is described as an in house closed off parenting style. It creates a disconnect from neighbours and those around us, where neighbours used to gather, there now exists an environment of solitude.

Earlier we mentioned society has moved away from church being so important in daily life. It has a direct influence on both our beliefs and family structure. As we shift away from religious ideology structuring our definition of family, we are seeing the passing of new ideas and new beliefs redefining the term "family". While the old faithful to the Biblical teachings stay true to their beliefs, the less religious are more likely to become increasingly openminded towards issues and will indeed reflect these differences in setting those family value systems.

Many things contribute to the family structure of each household. Single parent homes face all the same struggles of a two parent, home but face those adversities alone. Divorce is a common factor today, and the rate of divorce is moving higher each year. The argument could be made that with less influence from the Bible, more selfish behaviours and busy demands of today there exists less interest to work out differences. An argument could be made also that with the influence of the social media platforms, and with more online dating sites, people are simply falling for the "grass is greener on the other side", mentality. One trend that is troublesome is the frequency of how many parents are pushing new social issues upon their children. We saw not to long ago an eleven, year old boy, perform at gay strip clubs for adult males and had money thrown at him for this. ABC's Good Morning America did a segment on this family and focused on the support from his parents for being brave enough to be himself. What is troubling is that a parent would allow their child to dance/perform for money in strip clubs, let alone at his early age of eleven. You can support your son and his determination for being himself, you should have known better than to sexualize this and allow profit from it to happen.

We have also witnessed Drag Queen Reading Hour, where Drag Queens in full Drag read stories to children. The problem here is the story involved twerking and came with the Drag Queen showing the children how to twerk. Has decency dropped so low that we are alright with the sexualizing of our children? Other instances have been recorded of similar behaviour for birthday parties, and it is on the parents to ultimately decide if this is something that bothers them or, are they tolerant of children seeing this.

We have become a world where we have begun forcing our adult issues upon our children and are sexualizing them at early ages. Insinuating that babies are racist, or that small children are gay, trans or other such occurrences reserved for those old enough to understand and know, that face these issues daily, is wrong. In many instances, it reflects more about the parents than the children.

Chapter Seventeen
Words Matter

In today's world we are more than ever aware that words have meanings, and they do matter. This is the main reason that the Left and the Right clash so many times on wording or the way people choose to say how they feel. Often because the Right leaning are more inclined to use facts to back up their stance, where the Left are more feeling based, we see the term, "offended", used lots. It is incredibly difficult to argue or debate a subject when only one side is using the facts where the other is more wanting to talk about how it makes people feel. This is not to say that we should ignore other's feelings, or not account for others when we are speaking or debating. We must however, during debate or discussion about policy's remember it is important that the truth be used as the guideline.

The effectiveness of the mainstream media and the Left over the course of President Trump's time in office was due to repetitiveness of words. If we use our words to constantly describe someone in a negative fashion or use words that have negative meaning and attach them to how we describe others we can create an overall view that is negative. The mainstream media during the two and a half year coverage of the Muller report was effective in broadcasting a negative view of Donald Trump even though no proof had been presented. This was a helpful tactic for the Democrat party as it diminished the character of Donald Trump over the course of the entire investigation with the presumption of guilt without the burden of proof. The effective strategy of not declaring he was guilty but insinuated guilt by wording alleviated the mainstream media from having to issue an apology. Make no mistake there should have been many apologies issued as the strategy initiated by the mainstream media and the Democrat party showcased the coverage of the Muller investigation was indeed a political strategy. Reiterating the fact that if we hear something often enough it becomes completely believable even if it has not been proven to be truthful.

As mentioned, we see that social media offers an outlet that is oftentimes used in hurtful ways by the wording chosen. It allows us to use attacks that we may not be willing to do face to face, but because it is over the Internet, have found our nerve. This is often called trolling and many people will run into this kind of interaction on social media where trolls are simply there to say the worst possible things for reactions. The thrill for these, "so called" trolls is in the responses and arguments that is generated from their initial rude comment. This has led to the comment section being disabled on sites because of this trend.

Don Lemon took to CNN airwaves to call all 74 million Republican voters who supported Donald Trump racist and tolerant of the KKK. Lemon has also gone on record to say the biggest threat to America is white males that are radicalized to the right. Insinuating that anyone that is voting for the Republican Party must be radicalized and racist. This kind of wording is meant to create a stigma towards those people voting for the Republican Party in hopes of changing their vote to the Party Don Lemon supports. This kind of rhetoric should be illegal as it is an attempt to sway votes and those guilty of it should not be able to broadcast to the masses.

This leads me to the next section where often during debates or discussions that are feeling based versus fact based, questions, there is no real substance to back up your claims. Often what comes after some uncomfortable conversation, is personal attack of some kind from the side that can not support their claims. This lashing out is often an attack on the intelligence of those on the Right and calls into question their ability to comprehend truth. Most conservative minded Right leaning people are less interested in how people feel about the situation compared to the facts of the situation. Lashing out at another person because you have no answer, or you have mis-information about a subject, is not tolerable, or a mature way to end a discussion. It is OK to admit that you do not have all the information you need to form an opinion and admitting this will result in looking less foolish in the end.

The biggest offender of words matter are the media and the accountability that should be there to enforce more meaningful and accurate coverage. Being able to highlight an advantage for a political party that the news channel supports is not what journalism is defined as. Likewise, politicians at all levels should be very accountable for their words and the context to which they use them. The Biden Presidency along with the House and Senate wanting to impeach Donald Trump on inciting violence is rich after so many instances where they literally called for Left supporters to get into peoples faces and demand they be denied services. The Democrats not denouncing the riots and looting during the 2020 leadup to election night and setting up accounts to pay for bail to release those caught by police is disgraceful. Using words to incite or remaining silent during those times of violence is the same thing, as the latter is perceived as tolerance. During the 1955 NHL season Maurice "the Rocket" Richard was suspended for 3 games and the entire playoffs. The city of Montreal erupted into a riot, which would lead to Maurice Richard making an announcement on the radio for people to stop rioting. Why with all the technology of today did the Democrat Party members never once ask this of the rioters and looters creating chaos in the streets?

We must remember to use words that are not offensive when we discuss with others, and if we are willing to offend it showcases a lack of decency. If in debate or discussion heated points of contention come to a boiling point, it is best to move on to new subjects. Stopping to ask ourselves is it worth losing a friendship over or worth looking in poor character. The old saying of the pen being mightier than the sword is still true today. Using hurtful wording or personal attacks to try and win the last word in arguments or debates is never the right choice.

Perhaps the most fearful use of words today is in the form of labelling. With a nation so easily offended, and the existence of cancel culture, we are fearful of having our words twisted or misused and becoming labelled as a racist or xenophobe. One YouTube, video showed a woman being asked her age by a counter protester, to which she referred to him as an agist. Labelling people, we want to silence because they oppose our ideas is wrong, and sadly happens far to often today.

This is best illustrated by the mainstream media and Democrats labelling Donald Trump as racist, xenophobic, and many other words. The problem is the lack of proof, which further highlights the need for heavier accountability for our words. We have witnessed this also in townhall settings in Canada where Prime Minister Justin Trudeau upon being asked a question of financial burden for immigration policies. Trudeau had no answer for the woman asking him to explain where the financial help would be coming from, lashed out at her, calling her a racist, then walking out of the townhall meeting. All it takes is for others to uphold the label that is unfairly placed upon someone to make it take root.

The greatest use of wording to describe two different scenarios, yet similar events would be the Capital Riot and the protests during the last year. The Left leaning news media outlets showcased the fires and looting of businesses as "mostly peaceful" protests. The businesses destroyed and the amount of destruction that followed was catastrophic. The media would have you believe that these events are fine, and Chris Cuomo of CNN would even ask viewers, "where does it say protests have to be polite"? These same media outlets made the protests at the Capital into the most offensive and intolerable event ever. The truth, there is no tolerance for any riot, or looting period. Democrat Alexandria Ocasio-Cortez was accusing Republicans of almost having her murdered and was claiming she was afraid of protesters in the hallway outside her office. There was no one in the hallway outside her office, her office is on the other side of the road from where the protests occurred. Playing further into the wording issue, she claimed that the police officer that came to check on her was a source of fear for her, as she pushes for "Defund the Police". Where was AOC when the business owners were losing their livelihoods? Where was the Democrats in general? Tolerant of violence and backed by the Media to word it as peaceful.

Chapter Eighteen
Fear

Over the course of the last ten years, we have witnessed an alarming amount of change to the social fiber of both the United States and Canada. This change has not brought with it a better version of accountability or behaviour. Today sadly, we are confronted with the cancel culture, and the effective tool this culture uses is, fear.

Fear played a massive role in the Trump Presidency, as the media and Left would portray him as an untrustworthy, racist, xenophobic, and anti-women's rights, President. A President who conspired with a foreign country to steal the election of 2016 from Hillary Clinton, a President who hates people of dark skin colour, and Muslim countries. This fear would be broadcast daily, inundating viewers with negative coverage all the while telling them the end was near.

Fear plays a large role in the daily lives of almost every person in North America. We are afraid that our words might lead to someone misinterpreting what we are saying as inappropriate or offensive, and label us with one of many hate labels. Causing us to lower our voices when talking freely with others so that what we say is not overheard by anyone nearby. Some of the same labels were used against Mitt Romney when he ran against Obama for President, as were used against Trump.

Fear can silence us from speaking our minds, keep us from asking tough questions, and from getting the real answers about tough subjects. I return to the townhall where Justin Trudeau was asked how, are we going to pay for the large influx of refugees into Canada. Instead of answering the question, Trudeau resorted to lashing out at the woman and calling her a racist. The effectiveness of fear is in the ability of those using it to virtue signal that they are being the tolerant or better person, when in fact they are silencing opposition.

Fear is also the main factor that keeps people from wanting to even mention some subjects. No matter how important it is to discuss, and talk about key factors that build better communities, some people will remain silent and refrain from dialog. This is a contributor to how the Left gets away with many things that most people know to be wrong or in need of correcting, but sadly will not be called on out of fear. The best example is how the media refused to report that Trump had in fact denounced the KKK and White Nationalists, many times in fact. By refusing to report this fact, the media kept a narrative going that was untrue and out of fear, no one argued the point. Out of fear of being listed as a racist themselves, not many people would argue the point, and just like that, the Left made a racist out of a man who had contributed immensely to the black community.

Fear is also the main reason that Hillary Clinton was projected to win the 2016 election. With BLM outside of the polling stations, people felt afraid to answer questions honestly upon exiting and the information was unreliable, and incorrect. Fear is a strong campaign strategy, and it can keep people from sharing the reasons they support a candidate. This is what happened with Trump, as many people were attacked for supporting the Republican candidate and called or labelled negatively for any showcasing of that support.

There can be no tolerance of this stereotyping, for the use of fear to silence an idea we do not want to hear. When we rush to label people as racists or other negative connotations to describe, unlike minded people, we water down those people who are truly racist, and awful human beings. The media spent so much time and effort trying to compare Trump to Adolf Hitler, in order to tarnish his image, but only managed to bolster Trump supporters who could see through the lightly vailed attempts.

The largest problem in using fear as a silencer is the moment facts enter the equation, and can support stances, the Left usually resort to labelling or name calling through personal attacks. This highlights that most people are willing to cross a line with friends and strangers alike to attempt looking less foolish. Which reminds us that if we do not know the details of a subject, we should refrain from discussing it with those who do.

In order to strengthen our free speech, and to gain back the liberty and rights we possess as a people, we need to fight back against this fear mongering, and label applying culture. Hate is heard and recognized by everyone, we do not have to be told that something is racist because it could be taken this way or another. Do not give real racists and hateful people free passes on the vileness that exists out there because the wrong person won the election over your candidate. Instead, direct all the attention that gets directed at people like Donald Trump, towards actual monsters that live among us.

Chapter Nineteen
Double Standard

Now without a doubt, there is a double standard that exists in North America, and it is an aspect that desperately needs to go away. The double standard is two different sets of rules apply to the Left and Right Wing, political parties. Who sets these standards you might ask? Well, it is mainly the Mainstream Media, and the Democrats, themselves, but also those voters that refuse to hold those on the Left to more account.

Now the greatest illustration of this would undoubtably be the border crisis. Under President Trump the border was a main problem for the Democrat Party, even moving AOC to do a photoshoot at the fencing around the compound housing the would be, asylum seekers. The Democrats and the MSM would go on full tangent about the housing facility labelling it a "concentration camp" and referring to it as "kids in cages". The problem the Democrats had was the inhumane treatment these people were receiving, and the crowded space available. Now that President Biden is in power, somehow no one from the Democrat Party wants to go to the border or mention the alarmingly increased problem now facing the border. The MSM will not address it or push the issue nearly as much or with the same level of venomous hatred as they did with Trump. Neither Biden or Harris, are taking questions about the border, and no media releases are being given yet. So why are there such differences in the way the MSM reports the same issue, one incredibly more problematic, and the increase to the number of people housed in the facility 1000% higher under Biden? Why has the MSM now changed the name to a friendlier more positive name? Has the Democrats forgotten about the border, have they simply stopped caring about the inhumane treatment? The real problem is that these people are believing they will be let into the country, and that the border is completely open. And the name of the compound they eventually get housed in is irrelevant retrospectively. The issue is real, there is a crisis in the handling of the situation and no amount of misleading information, or lashing out from the Left, or the MSM renaming it as a friendly, happy place will change the fact that it is a crisis. Both the MSM and the Democrats should be ashamed of themselves for the portrayal during Trump's Presidency and the lack of real action to prevent the situation from worsening.

Double Standards exist in various areas where the public must form opinions. We are witnessing a wide range of issues lately and it is very much a full war between the Left and Right. The manner to which Brent Kavanaugh was treated concerning his behaviour from 30 years or more ago, verses how Biden, Cuomo, and Ellison have been treated about similar accusations. The media had a field day on the Kavanaugh accusation, with coverage being very extensive, while no real coverage of the Democrats that were being accused making the news at all. Why this double standard, are women's rights only a problem if Republican's are being accused? Does the impact on their lives change and become much less of an issue if Democrats are the accused? Well, the problem is perception, and the MSM build up the image of the Democrats all the while destroying the image of the Republicans it seems to me. Again, the best example of this is Alyssa Milano who was incredibly outspoken and angry during Kavanaugh's accusation but has remained completely silent about any of the Democrat situations. She is not the only celebrity or Left politician who has done so. Trump was subjected to incredibly poor coverage and scrutiny during his accusation from Stormy Daniels, and Amy Coney Barrett was even asked about abusing people sexually when she was appointed to the Supreme Court. With the MSM and Left giving free passes to the Democrats, it makes one believe it is more of a political strategy than concern for women's rights.

We should all be respectable towards one another, regardless of political party or affiliation, but we see that is not the case today. It appears to be open season on Conservatives, and this is best demonstrated by the way violence and physical assaults are carried out on them. The MSM helped present to the American public an image of negativity towards Conservatives, and in doing so, fueled the fires between the two sides. Labelling all followers of a Party as sympathisers of KKK or receiving zero pushback from the MSM when calling all things related to Right Wing issues as racist is absurd, and it needs to end.

Could you imagine the amount of coverage that would be present if instead of Biden's son being investigated for all the things that allegedly have happened, it was Trump's son? Imagine the time that would be allotted to a Republican that allowed a Chinese spy to infiltrate their office.

Perhaps the saddest double standard involves Mrs. Melania Trump, one of the most beautiful First Ladies to ever grace the White House. Melania is not an American born woman, she was born in Slovenia, and because of that, her first language is not English. She received a ridiculous amount of criticism over this issue from the beginning of Trump's run for President from Hollywood, Democrat and Mainstream Media alike. She was made fun of by large numbers of Left followers as well. If tolerance is a blessing the Left possess, and are always talking about acceptance why did they not champion a beautiful woman, smart and courageous, putting her child before herself and his concerns? She did not immediately move into the White House from where Barron was used to living, she was looking out for her son and the effects of the new direction their lives would be taking. These are admirable moves that only a genuine loving Mother would take to protect her children, not things that should be used as character assassination against her. Jill Biden destroyed the Spanish sentence she was trying to use to a crowd, and there was zero heard from the Left on it or the Right thankfully.

So why did Jimmy Kimmel need to make fun of Melania, or why did many in Hollywood feel they needed to follow suit? Why is it alright to attack Melania and not give her the cover of any magazine or the same type of acceptance as Democrat wives?

Could anyone imagine the MSM not condemning Republicans over riots that left large areas of cities destroyed? Could you imagine Republicans setting up accounts to help support those rioters, but not the businesses that are being destroyed? Well, these actions have transpired over the course of the build up to the 2020 election, and the MSM gave out hall passes to Democrats, even going so far as to broadcast fires burning while stating "mostly peaceful" protests. Or statements like, "who said protesters need to be polite?"

When one side is given a free pass on behaviours unbecoming of public office, or actions that do more damage than good we all lose. Those people should be removed from office or be forced to resign. With the aid of the MSM, and the twisting of the real facts of situations to make a narrative fit the Left, there remains a need for laws that hold more account to these organizations. When the MSM make more money off the negative portrayal of all things Right and cater to that group by changing the actual happenings, it is criminal. Maybe we will witness a change in laws in the coming years that will hold the MSM more accountable.

When Trump took office, he immediately changed his policies to oppose those of Barack Obama. Upon the success of this action, Trump's unemployment numbers plummeted, and his job creation skyrocketed. Leading many to say Trump had the best first term Presidency of any resent President. But Trump's triumphs would be claimed by Obama as his own, and many would also attribute those to Obama from the Left as well. Many MSM segments would be devoted to the coverage of Trump not being responsible for his own success. Now that Biden is in office and with 50 to 60 executive orders signed, we are witnessing the return to Obama like policies, and a surge at the border, surge in prices at gas stations, plummeting job creation, surge in unemployment. We are also witnessing people from the Democrat Party calling the surge at the southern border and the crisis all Trump's fault. So, when Trump wins the Left steals his credit, but when they fail, Trump gets the blame, and the media is not talking about this ridiculous behaviour.

Maybe the greatest visual of the double standard is how the two sides are permitted to exchange information with their followers. Censorship is something that the Left is not facing, and the Right is being silenced by big tech companies like Twitter, Facebook, and YouTube. Maxine Waters at the protests before the verdict was read during the Chauvin trial would tell protesters that they needed to become more confrontational, and to stay on the streets. During the lead up to the 2020 election, the Democrats did little, or almost nothing to prevent or quell the violence and looting riots. Now Donald Trump who told Senate and House GOP to go to the Capital and raise Hell, is not allowed to Tweet or be on Facebook. Why then is Maxine Waters allowed to continuously tell supporters to either approach Right supporters, or get more confrontational, escalating tensions, and potential violence, without any MSM coverage? LeBron James posted a picture of a police officer who saved a young teens life, from a knife carrying woman, with the caption, "you're next". He later deleted the Tweet, but not before it was shared over six thousand times. This officer saved the life of this girl, and he should not be subjected to this kind of mistreatment, doxing officers for doing their job is not something James should be doing.

An earlier point I made about the Ayatollah of Iran being able to Tweet nasty comments but President Trump being banned is ridiculous. It showcases a Party preference by the big tech companies, and it is designed to silence the Right message, or to hamper the ability to share information. It is designed to give the advantage to the Party that the big tech companies support. Why is Maxine Waters, or LeBron James not banned for inciting violence? Why is the Ayatollah not banned from Twitter for his comments clearly promoting hatred? The answer is clear, censorship is only one sided, and very much political in nature.

Let us focus on why censorship is key for the Left. The Left focus is squarely on the emotional connection with their base, and the

Right is rooted squarely in facts to base their stances. It is incredibly hard to debate facts with emotions, and it would be a great political strategy to silence the movement that can place facts before their support base. We see a new movement happening withing the North American environment where history itself is under attack. Quite literally people are trying to rewrite history and those prominent figures in it. Case in point in San Francisco they changed the high school named after Abraham Lincoln all because city council was unsure of his treatment of Indigenous people and the level to which he cared about African America people. By changing the historical happenings to fit narratives of today, we erase actual events.

The Democrats have long stated that the Republican Party of today was the Democratic Party of old when they opposed the voting rights, and freedoms for slaves. Twisting historical events to place negative aspects of their past onto their opponent is something we are seeing daily now. Censorship of the Right, and silencing their ability to relay those facts, coupled with a new historical version only the Left believes, is frightening.

A follower of the Democratic Party even went so far as to say the GOP made up the riots and looting in American cities over the 2019 – 2020 election cycle. Suggesting that the protests were best behaved protests in history, opening the door for misinformation, and a change to historical events to fit a narrative not based in truth or fact. This was merely his opinion, but a supporter of the Left might believe it and share that same stance with other like-minded people. Ignoring the facts and multiple video coverages of the riots, be led by a want and hatred of Trump to go along with the stance. It is his social media account, and he can post whatever he wishes, as a Leftist he has even more freedom to do so. Evident by no fact check label being placed under his statement to showcase the misinformation.

Chapter Twenty
Executive Order

Joe Biden has signed more than sixty Executive Orders, most reversing Trump's policies, and some addressing the Covid19 pandemic. These Executive Orders are a power that President's possess, and the manner to which Biden is going about the use of them is troubling. The reversal of policies that directly affect American workers livelihood is very troubling, and the lack of a plan to get them back into the workforce is equally troubling. Biden cancelled the Keystone Pipeline and permits for land exploration has caused prices to surge at pumps, costs to heat houses to surge, reliance on Arab nations oil to sustain needs to also increase. The need has not been changed or lessened by this Executive Order it has only changed the people who profit off the continuing need still present in America. Catering to the Climate Change voices, and the Left that want change as far as emissions, is a step in the right direction, but not with one single stroke of the pen. If only new jobs were created as easily. You can not cancel jobs by the thousands and still have a need for the product those jobs provided and declare victory. New jobs, and an actual plan would alleviate prices skyrocketing, dependence on other countries supply, and unemployment numbers rising.

The use of so many executive orders to start off Biden's Presidency is to avoid going through the Senate and House to get policy passed. I feel it is a direct result of passing policy that would stand zero chance of passing if given a vote in either the House or Senate.

Not many Presidencies have started out with so many Executive Orders signed, and I think that those changes that will be brought about because of these orders, will change the country for the worse. Not just the job killing that cancelling the Keystone Pipeline will bring, but also the cancelling of the border wall construction. With the end of construction on the wall, the surge has a large area to come into the country and has made the crisis we see today. The message sent that we are open by the Biden administration, and cancelling of the wall, has given those wanting to come to America the idea that it will be a "walk on in", without any questions approach. Yet within the first three months of Biden's Presidency neither Biden nor Harris has visited the border, and within that same timeframe have blamed Trump and refuse to call it a crisis. What the stroke of a pen can do is indeed alarming, what that pen can do in the wrong hand, one without any follow up plan is even more alarming.

Rejoining the Paris climate agreement is not entirely bad, however, paying large sums of money that could be used elsewhere is poor governance. Allowing undocumented immigrants to be included in census, but not arranging proper paths to fix the undocumented immigrant from taking the proper channels to become legal citizens is wrong.

Keeping the country safe is first and foremost, and lifting travel bans on countries that are known hotbeds of terrorism is not a safe plan, it looks to be a nice gesture but little else. Biden has lifted the travel ban on Muslim countries but placed a ban on Brazil and most of Europe. This is nothing better than virtue signalling, travel bans should be to protect the people from a virus, not distinguish race or religion into the factor.

We all know that it is crucial to the vitalization of industry that apprenticeship programs be put in place. Biden with the stroke of a pen has rescinded a Trump order that would expand apprenticeships. In so doing, will leave America to depend on either those jobs being outsourced to other countries like China or Mexico, or bringing in immigrants to do the work here. Instead of expanding the apprenticeship to give those jobs to our youth here, this is the wrong path for future sustainability.

Biden also revoked an order Trump issued that would hold back funds to cities that allow anarchist behaviour, an example would be the 100+ days Seattle allowed "chop" to be set up causing a man to lose his life in the process. Only after the life was lost did the city move to disperse the area. What this order does is bolster the support of those rioters and looters that take to the streets and cause chaos.

The Democrat Party was incredibly angry and upset by the appointment of both Judge Kavanaugh and Judge Barrett to the Supreme Court. By Executive Order Biden wants to study possible reforms allowing the Democrats to pack the SCOTUS from nine members to thirteen members. This is a move that would place the majority in favour of Left supporting Judges giving the advantage to the Democrat side. The SCOTUS should not be a place where Political Party affiliation is a deciding factor in the matter of Law decisions. This move is nothing more than political and is unconstitutional.

A new call to abolish the Electoral College is coming forward from the Left, and this would destroy the chances of mid-America having a say in any future election. The Electoral College has been in place since the 1800's, and changes to that platform would make areas of the United States less important on election day. This move would be shameful and hopefully it never happens and would not be something that could be done through Executive Order without many States bringing it before the courts.

With the Executive Orders that Biden has signed already, the course of the United States has changed from the successful path Trump was traveling. The change is leading the country back to the failures of the Obama era and will further cement the fact that Trump's success was not Obama's work. What is something Obama will be able to claim is the same failures that will plague the Biden/Harris administration, as they are the same failures of his administration.

Executive Orders are something that President's use to set the path for their term. Many Presidents have utilized this power, and some have issued a large, number of orders. What the list of orders that Biden has signed allow is the troubling issue, and what it will bring as far as detriment to the working people of the United States of America with it, is staggering. People need work to be able to live, earn money, provide for their family, and feel like they contribute to society. Trump had the unemployment in Black and Hispanic people at an all time low and was bringing more jobs back before the pandemic hit. With Biden cancelling jobs in many sectors like construction and natural resources it will bring about a dependency on Government handouts like unemployment and welfare. Once the unemployment term runs out on those workers, without any plan to create jobs in the immediate future, they will be left with no course of action but to go on welfare and food stamps. This is what happened during Obama's Presidency as well, the number of people leaving the workforce was incredibly high. The fact that when workers are leaving the workforce they no longer are counted among the unemployed, and a false number is created where it looks like the number of people working is getting better. The reality though, is the situation is more dire than it appears, and sadly this will be what happens a year from Biden taking office.

Executive Order that Biden should have signed into power would limit the amount of trade and interaction the USA has with China. Both for China's climate contributions being ridiculously high, with zero regard for changing their emissions, and for the inhumane treatment of the Uyghur people. Yet sadly Biden has not denounced China and is yet to really address the genocide happening there. Pulling out of the Olympics would be a great start to show the world that inhumane treatment will not be tolerated.

Chapter Twenty-One
Moving Forward

So how are we going to correct these wrongs and change to bring about the unity Joe Biden is now calling for. Well, we are never going to achieve that unity calling for uncivil behaviour if we lose elections. This behaviour is a formula for how you achieve the opposite of unity. Using a call to be uncivil as a political strategy needs to be punishable by law, as we have witnessed over the course of the 2020 election how devastating it can be. The call for unity should never be issued only after gaining power or used as a tool to get it.

After the 2020 election a few members of the Democrat Party were calling on obtaining a list of Trump voters. This is illegal and would only serve those on the Left a complete list of people to attack to prevent future votes going Republican. With calls to have Trump or Republican voters reprogrammed a list of those voters would be incredibly harmful to any unity at all.

Silencing voices will in fact create less opportunities to grow and eventually come around to create an environment where no one will be allowed to speak freely. Both sides are entitled to a voice and an opinion, neither side of the political game should want this to happen. Much like irregularities in the voting system if they exist should be addressed. Both sides should want a fair and just election to determine the leader of the country.

We must work on an agenda of bettering the country not one of bettering a Party, or personal objectives. JFK once said, "let us not seek the Republican answer or the Democratic answer, but the right answer". This is something that has gotten away from the Democratic Party over the last few years. Working so hard to oust a President that was popular and voted into office fairly is not the way to achieve unity.

Remarks of Senator John F. Kennedy at the Loyola College Annual Alumni Banquet, Baltimore, Maryland, February 18, 1958. (February 18, 1958). https://www.jfklibrary.org/archives/other-resources/john-f-kennedy-speeches/baltimore-md-19580218

Many States will be working on fixing problems they feel existed in the voting process during the 2020 election. Were there, irregularities in the 2020 election process? Will any changes be made to how people vote in the next election? Ensuring that a fair, and legitimate outcome be the deciding factor in selecting the highest office in the country should be paramount to any political differences that exist. In every election there arises those issues, be it small or large, that deserve attention. The desired result of bettering the process should always be at the forefront, and those issues should be examined after the election. And this is just one thing that needs to be addressed.

Creating more jobs for the everyday American will limit the amount of dependency they have on Government. With this liberation comes less likelihood of a political Party using you as a pawn and having you do the dirty work like rioting and looting to illustrate a sense of unrest that would not have been there.

Hold the Mainstream Media accountable far more often and set guidelines to visit stories after they are reported. Creating a board that will use the same set of rules for all News channels and be responsible for handing out fines if those guidelines are broken. This is not to say infringe on freedom of speech or freedom of expression but create an environment where people can once again trust the news they are receiving. This will eliminate the helping of one political Party over another with how and what is broadcast to American homes.

Way more needs to be done as far as holding Parties accountable for their actions. What we have witnessed from 2016 to 2021 already is not the best of the Democratic Party of America. From attacking the President continuously with zero proof and even continuing after Trump has left office is shameful. A willingness to destroy a man's name and character for political power is nothing short of evil, and if it was just Trump, it might go unnoticed. If there is no respect or line that will not be crossed to gain power, it will only lead to both Parties playing the same game. When the outcome is obtained by who can out cheat each other, everyone loses.

The Parties must do a better job of holding those fellow members accountable for what they do and say, if not, it will only make the Party look corrupt and pathetic. Remembering that you align yourself with the Party and if those representing the Party act in a manner unbecoming of elected office, you bear their discretion with them. If those members of the Democratic Party were not angered by Hillary accepting the questions to the debate with Trump, they showcase their lack of indignation towards unfair, and wrong behaviour.

I want to say that just because I do not support the Democratic Party, or the policies that they put forward as a Party, that does not mean I think their policies are 100% wrong. I understand that many people feel these policies are the correct course of action needed for today's world. I am not against any movement in the United States that builds up communities, or against Black Lives Matter movements. I 100% support the LGBTQ+, and disavow all forms of hatred, be that KKK or any form that leads to hate. I openly research all religions to justify to myself my own faith, and to learn where people of other religions and I can debate freely the many interesting points. Leadership today looks a little like it used to and needs to change to meet those things that make us who we are today. No where is there room for hatred in today's world, even my disapproval of the behaviour I have written about in this book is not from a hate, but disagreement with decisions. I understand we are all different, that is what makes us human.

Leadership from the younger members of both Parties is essential. Not just because of their age but those individuals that showcase true leadership qualities like Jim Jordan, Candace Owens, or

Tulsi Gabbard. Keep in mind these things written in this book are my opinions of how these people acted in their elected roles. I pass no judgement on their individual behaviour, only offer what I think they did that I disagree with, and what needs to change in order to move forward. The biggest thing needed to move forward is to find unity not just use the word as a slogan. Unity will take both sides working together, find the right leaders and representatives in the House and Senate and you will come together again.

Lightning Source UK Ltd.
Milton Keynes UK
UKHW010122300721
388013UK00006B/484/J